the *global* issue

Culture is the arts elevated to a set of beliefs.

>> Thomas Wolfe

FEATURES

Teaching Across the Globe

Insights, Local Challenges, and Inspiration from Educators All Around the World

34

Viva Africa

Graphic Decor Inspiration and Sources for a Unique, Global Home Aesthetic

24

Wander the World on a Teacher Budget

Tips for Travel, Customized Specifically for Teachers

52

CONTENTS

Geography Idea Hub
72

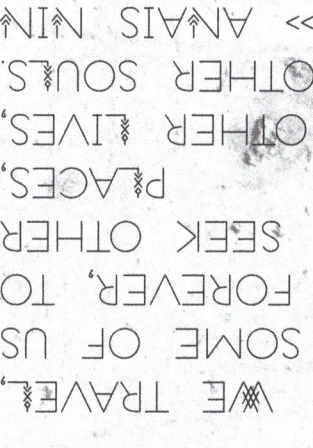

Adventures in "Unschooling"
12

» WE TRAVEL, SOME OF US FOREVER, TO SEEK OTHER PLACES, OTHER LIVES, OTHER SOULS. — ANAIS NIN

IN EVERY ISSUE

From the Editor	4
Bell Work	7
School Tour	38
Discover	50
Passing Notes	70
Mind of a Creator	76
Inspiration From...	96

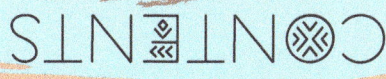

Teachers Are Artisans	10
How to Create a Cozy Home	60
Wanderlust + Creativity = Art	76
Faith-Fueled Teaching	80
Aboriginal Dot Art	84
New School: Rooted in Values & Nestled on a Bio-Dynamic Farm	88
5 Ways to Style an Oversized Cardigan	92

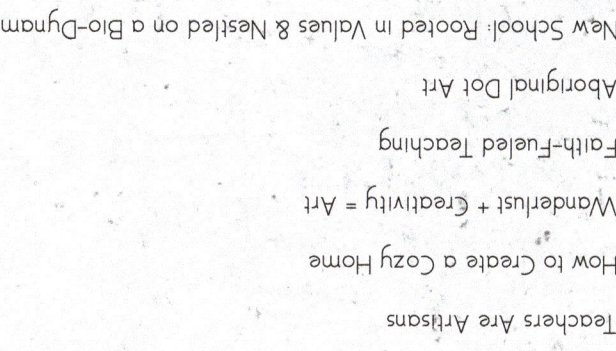

a global perspective

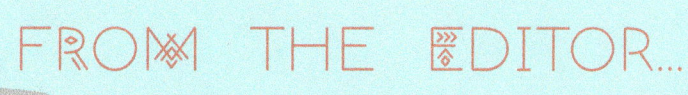
FROM THE EDITOR...

All across the globe, we share certain aspects of humanity. We're one human family, and many things are universal. But now that we are more connected than ever and have access to stories from all over the world, we can see such beautiful variation as well. In this issue, our goals are both sharing that beauty and learning from other cultures.

We've worked with educators from a wide range of countries and continents to give us a peek into different classrooms around the world. We've gathered information straight from each source on the ground and in the schools. Our central *Teaching Across the Globe* feature is all about the challenges of teaching in each area, as well as the upsides from which we can all draw inspiration. Some of the problems are issues that all teachers and schools have in common, while some are specific local struggles that may surprise you. But we also asked each teacher for the positive aspects. What is each country doing right that we can all learn from?

In addition to learning about education-based culture, we're sharing some lifestyle content from different places around the world as well. We're admiring the beauty of African home decor and showing you where to go to support the creators. We're looking at fair trade that supports artisans in a variety of countries. We've rounded up strategies from a wide range of teachers, homeschoolers, and even unschoolers to help you teach geography, art, and culture from far-off places in your classroom, and also incorporate the earth's diverse beauty into your home and personal life.

Of course, all this talk of global beauty from each different land is sure to make you want to travel, meet the people, and learn about the wide variety of cultures, so we are giving you some tips for wandering the world on a teacher budget.

Throughout this issue, we've also sprinkled in some concepts that originate from different countries and offer a new perspective. We hope that you will enjoy your relaxing time with this issue and will learn something new, gain fresh insights, appreciate the beauty and diversity of our earth and its incredible people, and find some fuel for your own soul.

Let Snowday be your guide to a productive, thoughtful, passionate
life as an educator AND as a
creative, vibrant human soul!

– Brigid

Spotlight Theme in this Issue: "Global Perspective"

Learn from the cultural beauty and the differences as well as shared experiences from all around the globe. We're exchanging information and inspiration with a wide variety of diverse teachers in this issue. Grab some classroom ideas from another region, get global decor and style insights, and take a moment for some big picture reflection in the special bonus pages where we pause to share a beautiful concept and term from a particular culure that can apply to all of humanity. These are interspersed throughout this issue to offer global perspectives we can all appreciate.

Photo: Avvy from The Muddly Puddly Laboratory @muddly_puddly (featured on p. 73)

Editor & Publisher
Brigid Danziger

Editing & Proofreading
Michael Dober

Writers
Kelly Barendt
Brigid Danziger
Vienna Rose
Carmen Myer

Sponsored and Produced by
Math Giraffe, LLC

Follow On Instagram
@snowdaymagazine

Contact Us
editor@snowdaymagazine.com

Advertising
media@snowdaymagazine.com

Website
SNOWDAYMAGAZINE.COM

Copyright 2021.

All rights reserved. Views, comments, and suggestions do not necessarily represent those of the publisher, and are provided as is. Snowday's editor and publisher disclaim any and all legal responsibility for the reader's use of any information included in this publication. Content given is not intended as a replacement for consulting an expert.

No portion of this publication may be reproduced without permission.

BELL WORK

Take a moment to set up text replacement shortcuts on your phone. You'll be glad you did every time they save you from having to retype a commonly used URL, message response, or your email address. It's especially handy to have these for things you type that have symbols and a combination of letters and numbers.

Of course, you'll need to choose shortcuts that you would not normally type as words or initials.

Examples:
cwp >> URL for class web page
sem >> school email address
pem >> personal email address

iPhone:
Settings > General > Keyboard > Text Replacement
Add new shortcuts by tapping "+," inserting the full URL, message, or address into the "phrase" field, and the shortcut you'd like to type to represent it in the "shortcut" field. Save.

Android:
Settings > Language & Input > Keyboard > Text Shortcuts (or Text Correction, depending on the device) > Add

creating & CONTRIBUTING

kalos

Kalos, the word for "beauty" in original Greek is literally translated to mean "beautiful as a sign of inward goodness."

This lovely phrasing expresses that beauty is not just about the aesthetics. It's a way of going through life and passing through the world.

To live beautifully is to live a life that contributes to human flourishing.

In our creative work, in our teaching, in our relationships, and in our communities, we can strive toward beauty as a sign of inward goodness.

TEACHERS are *artisans*

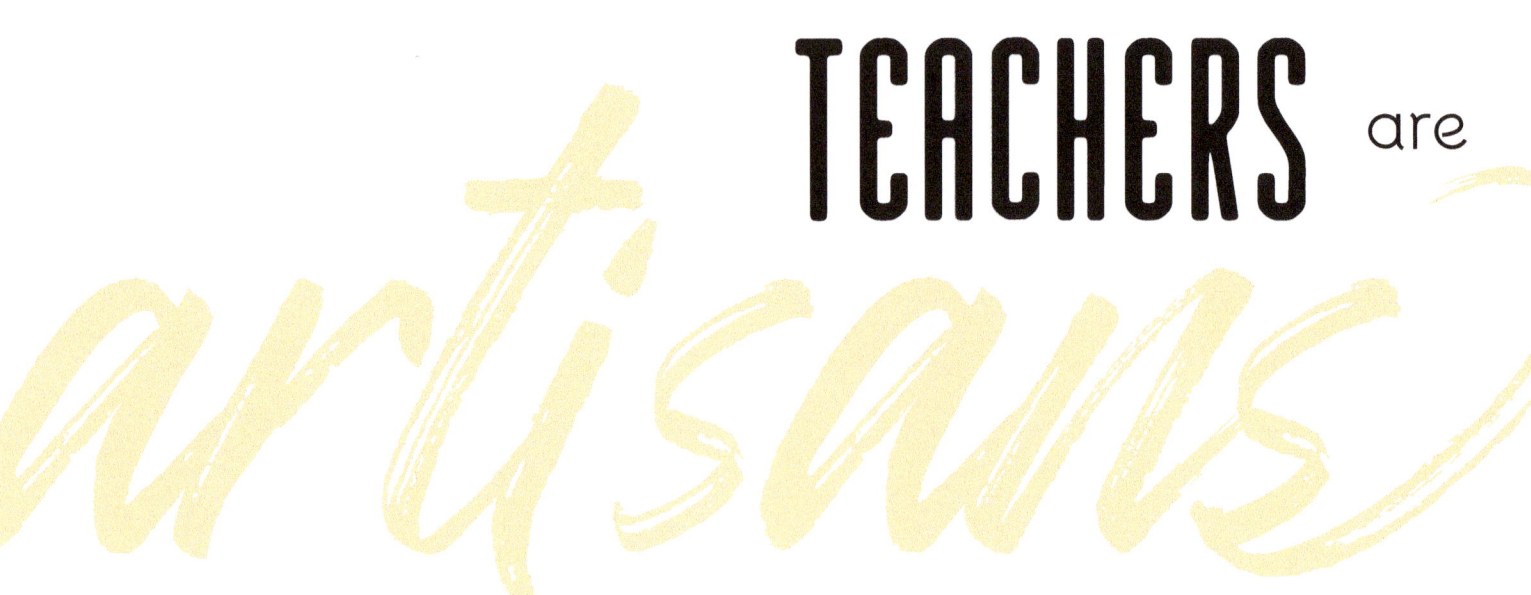

Artisans are craftspeople, skilled in their trades. There is no doubt that teaching is a craft that requires a delicate balance of many skills.

But one of the earliest translations of the term *artisan* comes from the past participle of the Latin word artitus, which meant "instruct in the arts," linking the word artisan not only to skilled handiwork, but also to education.

As teachers, we have a great role in passing on creativity. We craft lessons, we craft relationships, and we tend to even get crafty with our classrooms and organization. But in addition to the skilled work we do all day teaching and using our own creativity, we *instruct* our students in their own skills and help them to develop and nurture their own ingenuity.

Weavers in Peru are some of the most incredible artisans on earth. Every stitch, different pattern, and even the colors that are used each have great meaning. The weaver embeds significant information into their handiwork. The textiles are woven into graphic displays of their stories, ideas, and history to pass on to the next generation.

They are woven as a form of instruction for the little ones to learn from.

Like teachers, their skill in their craft is not just a beautiful artform and a marvel to see in action. It's also instructional. Just like classroom educators, the best artisans pass on the best of their history, their culture, and their dedication as part of their legacy to teach the next generation.

Many artisans pass on much more than they realize, and the impact of the work grows the more they perfect their craft.
Teach like an artisan.

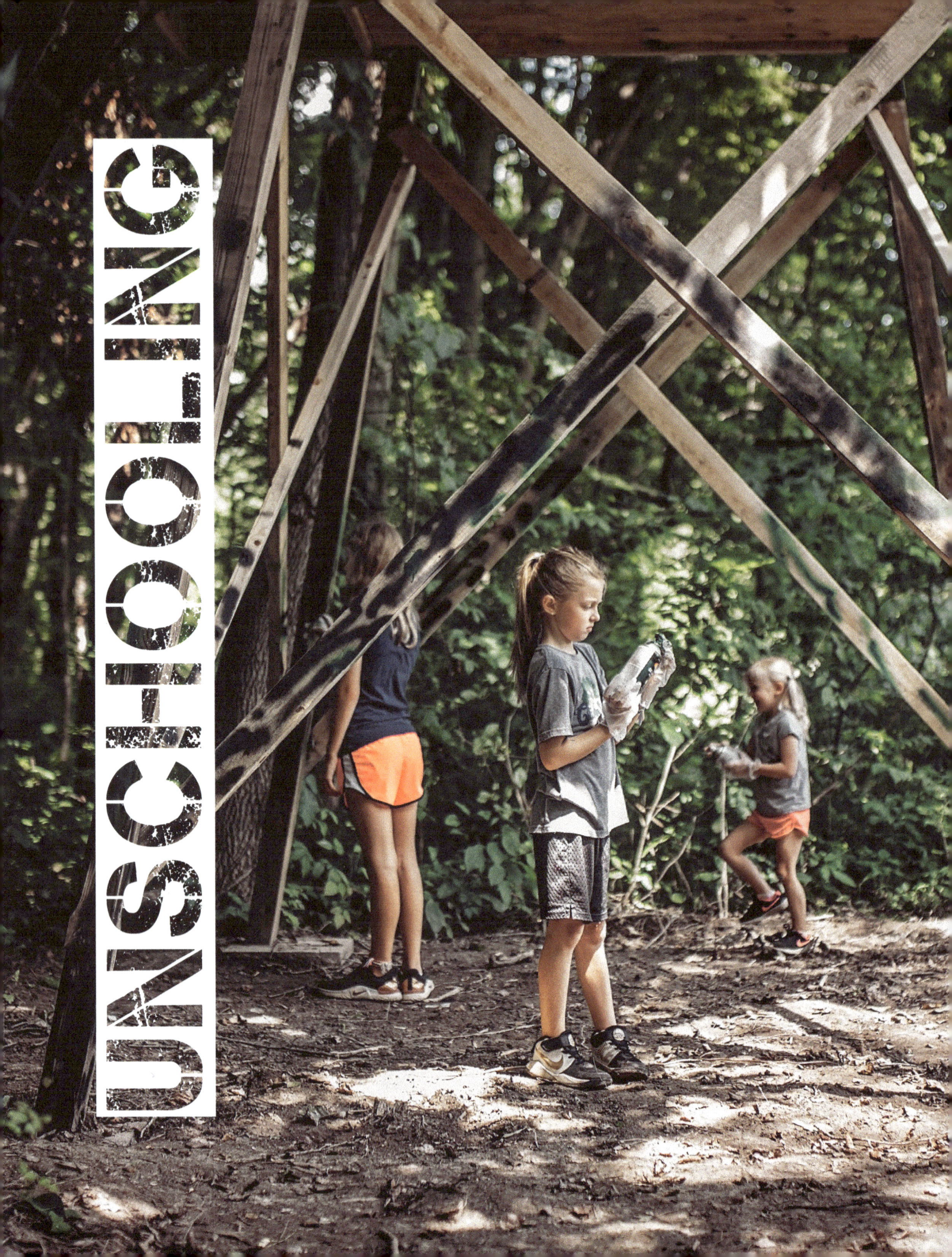

> It's incredibly important to nurture what lights their fire and I think it's our job to help them navigate it.

Adventures in "Unschooling"

by Caryn DeFreez
@caryndefreez

"freedom to nurture what stirs their souls"

The Journey to "Unschooling"

I had researched homeschooling for over a decade and I let the fear of not being adequate enough stop me from pursuing it. A few years ago, I was longing for a different lifestyle and wanting a different childhood for my children. They always say, "you only have 18 summers, make the most of it." UGH, I hated that saying. I wanted 18 years.

A client of mine turned friend reached out to me and said, "My friend Myah homeschools. I'd be glad to send you her info. She'd be glad to answer any questions." I'll never forget it. I was sitting in the Middle School pick up line waiting for my daughter when I made the phone call. Though we had never met in person, Myah made me feel like an old friend and she so graciously answered all of my questions. That one conversation was so powerful that I pulled my children the following week. Myah has continued to be a guiding light over the years.

I started out replicating the public school system at home. I had certain subjects taking place at certain times of the day and by 3pm, school stopped. I quickly learned that didn't fit our lifestyle, so I begin writing in notebooks. I would write a list of things they had to do for the entire week and they had all week to do the work. It was curriculum based, filled with worksheets and busy work. They were doing it just to get it done but not retaining any of the information. I stumbled upon unschooling and it changed our world. No more strict schedules or busy work. My children began thriving in this new lifestyle. Educating at home has its seasons just like anything else. As our children get older, certain things need shifting and thankfully, unschooling allows us that freedom to nurture what stirs their souls.

Homeschooling ultimately turned into unschooling simply because we wanted to take our freedom to learn a step further. The decision to stick with it came from seeing the results first hand. Of course there are rough days, days where you question if you are good enough to teach your children. Having a circle of friends who also homeschool / unschool that you can reach out to really helps during those off days.

Strategies for Success

You unschool every single day. Often, people don't consider learning or teaching if it isn't done in four walls, under a certified teacher or in some formal school. I always challenge parents to start creating a log of what they did each day along with what their kids might have learned or done for the first time, questions they asked and so on. Parents teach their kids to eat with spoons, crawl, walk, say words, and pick up toys, but suddenly at age five they assume they can no longer teach their kids anything. This couldn't be further from the truth. I think the world is evolving and the use of technology has really created an outlet for those who want to consider this lifestyle.

Journaling about our day and what they learned along with documenting the moments through pictures has been my go-to strategy for over a year now. Unschooling isn't necessarily about having curriculum, so it can be hard to track what they've done. When you can't track, you begin to question yourself: if you're doing the right thing, if it's enough, and if it's really working. Whenever I feel this way, I open up a journal or go out to my Instagram to view all of the images full of so many things we've accomplished.

My children also have a weekly log where they can write in things they've done each day along with things they are interested in learning. I find allowing them to write down their thoughts creates a drive for answers. They end up "doing school" without realizing it, so it's a win / win.

Priorities

Work ethic and communication are at the top of the list. We are a country family and there are always chores to be done. We've instilled in our children the need to "help out" without being told to do so. When they see a job needs to be done, they do it. They don't hesitate to jump in when they see others could use a hand. We want them to see the correlation between hard work and results.

Communication is a huge one around here. We talk all things tone, attitude, knowing the recipient, email communication, texting, and person to person conversation. Often, things get lost in translation or we assume a person understands, but that's not always the case. We want them to understand that the things they say and how they say them can create drastically different outcomes.

Try this: Have your child write down the directions on how to make a peanut butter and jelly sandwich. Have them watch you as you read and do exactly what they said in the directions. Not only will it be funny for them, but it's also eye opening. They'll forget things like "use the knife to scoop out a bit of peanut butter and spread that on one piece of bread." Instead they'll say "put the peanut butter on one side and jelly on another." You'll pick up the jar of jelly and literally put it on the piece of bread. We then discuss how being effective and proficient in communication can really change a scenario.

We are a family full of farmers and hunters. Land to run on is plentiful. We have quite a few chickens and we seem to keep acquiring more. We often joke that we aren't sure why we have a house because we don't spend much time in it. We spend a lot of time sitting in the garage watching the kids play or out in the woods helping put up deer blinds for the upcoming season or checking trail cams. Any time spent outdoors is time well spent. You'll often find our kids sitting on the back patio with a notebook researching whatever they are currently interested in or coloring pictures with chalk in the drive. From the time they wake up until we go to bed, most of our life and learning is done outside. They've been involved in helping with the chores or duties outside since they were little. It's now just become part of who we are. There's that saying, "There's no wifi in the woods, but I promise you will find a better connection." It's the truth and we know being outside has impacted our children in incredible ways.

W Watching my children discover who they are in their own time, without the pressure to be someone else... that's what this lifestyle is all about.

Life and Soul Inspiration

The journey to motherhood wasn't easy for me. Our girls were all born prematurely and we lost two of our sons who were born stillborn. I vowed to live this beautiful life I'd been given with intention.

I wake up each day with a clean slate and I aim to live each day like tomorrow is not promised.

It's easy to get caught up in the rat race of life, in social media, and in trying to keep up. We correlate being busy with success and that couldn't be any further from the truth. I know a lot of super busy people who seem to be falling apart.

We must slow our lives down, and be more intentional about our goals, dreams, and our family lives. After all, we work each day to provide a beautiful life for our family and we must take the time to LIVE IT, intentionally.

Motherhood is what fills my soul, hands down. I knew from an early age that my goal in life wasn't focusing on what college I wanted to attend or what job I was going have. I wanted to be a mom, period. I had incredible role models in my own mother and in her mother. I talk about it often on my Instagram, but I really believe that among all things in life, love and connections make the world go 'round. With both of those things, the possibilities are endless.

I think that's why education at home really appealed to me. Not every child has this inner drive to go off to college to be the doctor, nurse, or lawyer. I think it's incredibly important to nurture what lights their fire and I think it's our job to help them navigate it.

We love to explore new places. We've found the best learning experiences happen when we are on the road in our travel trailer, camping, hiking, or enjoying the Great Outdoors. Being able to see with your own eyes and learn about something in person is an experience you won't forget.

Watching my children discover who they are in their own time, without the pressure to be someone else... that's what this lifestyle is all about.

We must slow our lives down, and be more intentional about our goals, dreams, and our family lives. After all, we work each day to provide a beautiful life for our family and we must take the time to LIVE IT, intentionally.

13 Being able to see with your own eyes and learn about something in person is an experience you won't forget.

Creative Passions

I've been a photographer for nearly 12 years. I've photographed just about everything, but my heart quickly fell in love with documenting childhood. Last year, I took a break to really do some soul searching. Owning a business and unschooling children can be a lot, but I was determined to find a balance so I could also feed my own soul.

I decided to niche into documentary photography and in doing so, I started documenting our life, travels, adventures, and schooling. It's been a beautiful experience and has been an amazing way for me to document their education while also providing the creative outlet I needed.

If you need to prioritize your own creative outlet, do it! When you do what you love, you'll find a way to make time for it. Prioritize and understand that nurturing a craft/hobby is part of taking care of your soul. I always say "you can't pour from an empty cup." The time you take to nurture your own hobbies will ultimately pour over into your everyday life.

Thoughts for All Teachers:

First: Thank you, truly. Teachers, whether you're in public schools, in private schools, or are moms and dads being the teachers in your own homes, know that what you are doing is the world's greatest work.

Second: Get outside. I know that doesn't seem like a hack or trick, but it is. I can't tell you how many moms have said to me, "he just won't focus, he's not interested." I always respond, "take the work outside." I'm telling you, there's something about Mother Nature that is freeing and changes the mood.

trouvaille

The joyful French term "trouvaille" represents unexpected delight. Travelers feel it when they are ambling along as tourists and suddenly step through a small, but intricate archway on a peaceful street only to stumble into a hidden courtyard packed with the bustle of a beautiful local street market, surrounded by ancient stone walls, iron balconies, and a jungle of live foliage. While admiring the cafe lights strung up above the merchants' tents, the traveler would feel delighted with the unexpected find.

The lucky, but wonderful concept of trouvaille offers a feeling of surprise. By chance, sometimes we find a delightful but unexpected pocket of joy in life. It can be anything from a single flower blooming on a bush in your yard that you thought had died completely years ago to a piece of good fortune that lands in your lap. Consider it a gift, take a moment to marvel at it, and then just enjoy! Soak in the delight of an accidental find.

wonder & chance

Viva AFRICA

TEXT: MANDY ALLEN
PRODUCTION: SHELLEY STREET
PHOTOGRAPHS: WARREN HEATH
VIA BUREAUX

The starting point when introducing a touch of Afrique style into your home begins, always, with baskets. Functional as well as decorative, this exquisite piece with its bright handiwork illustrates the sophisticated direction that African craft is taking and how beautifully it integrates into contemporary spaces.

DECOR INSPIRATION

Graphic Africa

When the vibrant prints of the African continent are united with modern industrial design, the resulting aesthetic is one that is graphic, cosmopolitan, and electrifyingly directional. Bring the look home with beautiful baskets, tribal beadwork, and colorful textiles.

The Dark Arts

A dramatic wall shade remains one of the most effective backdrops against which to highlight furnishings, art, and accessories as well as instantly suggest an edgy urban mood. Here, an eclectic fusion of African textiles and hand-crafted objects sourced from across the continent including Swaziland, Central Africa, South Africa, and West Africa combine harmoniously with bespoke shelving and contemporary design, lending the space a Global Chic edge as well as warmth. Statement pieces in solid pops of color such as the occasional table, stool, and Klein blue vase serve to further highlight and connect with the distinctive patterns.

This fresh approach to decorating with African textiles and craft in combination with contemporary furnishings goes deeper than surface aesthetics and is essentially about a play on textures: smooth steel furniture and woven raffia baskets, cool marble surfaces and waxy oiled cloth, nubbly unglazed ceramics and glossy blown glass, luxe rugs and cheap-and-cheerful plastic mats.

* Selection of cushions made up in various wax cloth and batik-print fabrics from Mnandi Textiles. & Design (Facebook / Mnandi Textiles. Also see Vlisco: vlisco.com)
* Mustard-coloured throw, from @Home (home.co.za)
* Blue small stool/table, from Chair Crazy (chaircrazy.co.za)
* Sofa, Rug, Coconut Planters, and Marble-topped occasional tables, from Weylandts (weylandts.co.za)
* Black and white hand painted bowl by Martine Jackson, Black and white ceramic vessel by Lisa Firer, Small black vessel, Small blue telephone wire vessel, and beaded bowl from Africa Nova
* Large woven pot-shaped vessel with yellow lip, large woven platter/bowl, and Zig-zag river reed woven utility baskets from Design Afrika (designafrika.co.za)
* Natural/blue pendant shade (used as decoration), from Ashanti Design (ashantidesign.com)
* Animal figurines, for similar Ridlheim (rialheim.co.za)
* Horns, from Weylandts: weylandts.co.za (for similar ceramic horns, Ceramic Matters: Facebook / Ceramic Matters)
* Selection of baskets and bowls, Africa Nova
* Rosenthal Pacific Vibes vase by Christine Rathman, Hourglass Time Multi-coloured glass vessel (on bottom shelf), Footed Bowl (multi blue/black), Hay Kaleido Tray by Clara von Zweigbergk, Milano Bouquet Green/ Transparent Vase by Ichendorf, and Milano Bouquet Green/ Transparent Vase by Ichendorf, from Guild (theguildgroup.co.za)
* Coral-coloured side table, from Chair Crazy (chaircrazy.co.za)
* Natural planters, Stark Ayres (www.weylandts.co.za)

BEAUTIFUL HANDCRAFTED AFRICAN BASKETS AND QUIRKY OBJECTS THAT REFLECT THE RICHNESS OF THE CONTINENT'S WILD LANDSCAPES BRING A FRESH PERSPECTIVE TO A DISPLAY OF BOOKS ON A MODERN SHELVING SYSTEM. A MULTITUDE OF PLANTS EVOKES THE SENSE OF AN INDOOR JUNGLE.

The Clash

Your mission, should you choose to accept it, involves mixing and matching as broad a combination of colorful African prints and patterns as you please – in the form of both textiles as well as the gorgeous basketry and woven wire work that is so pervasive in African craft. While the rules of restraint don't apply to this look, there are a few style tricks you can follow that will keep the mood sophisticated. Punctuate the scene with black and white accents to allow the eye to rest amongst the abundance of color and pattern. While there's no need to be exacting about it, keep a balance between textiles with geometric patterns such as checks, stripes, and zig-zags and those sporting more discernible prints such as florals, swirls, and abstracted shapes.

* Large telephone wire basket (on top shelf) and Small woven basket from Africa Nova
* Blue small stool/table, from Chair Crazy (chaircrazy.co.za)
* Woven plastic rug and Zig-zag river reed woven utility baskets from Design Afrika (www.designafrika.co.za)
* Relax Occasional chair, from Waylandts (www.weylandts.co.za)
* Drum lampshade and cushion made up in batik fabric and Selection of cushions made up in various wax cloth and batik-print fabrics from Mnandi Texiles & Design Facebook / Mnandi Textiles. Also see Vlisco (vlisco.com)
* Blue small stool/table, from Chair Crazy (chaircrazy.co.za)

Geometry Lesson

In any decorative scheme, it's the objects that catch the eye that give it character. Every piece of African basketry comes with an emotive provenance, its value lying not only in the vibrant colors and patterns, but also the artistic expression and hand of its maker.

* Acrobatic pendant, Gamma stained oak dining table, and Swing Dining Chairs in black, from Waylandts (waylandts.co.za)
* Large woven pot-shaped vessel with yellow lip, from Design Afrika (designafrika.co.za)
* Black and white hand painted bowl by Martine Jackson and beaded bowl from Africa Nova
* Ichendorf Green Smoke Tequila Sunrise jug and Milano Bouquet Amber/Transparent Vase by Ichendorf, from Guild (theguildgroup.co.za / ichendorfmilano.com)
* Placemats made up in selection of fabrics, from Mnandi Textiles & Design (Also see Vlisco - vlisco.com)
* Recycled sandblasted glass tumblers, from Made in SA (waterfront.co.za / Made in SA)
* Blue plate, from Pick n Pay (pnp.co.za)

Industrial Evolution

In this composition, the vibrancy and handmade feel of the African objects give a refreshed feel to familiar industrial architectural elements such as exposed electrical piping, raw painted brick, and concrete flooring as well as mid-Century style chairs and a striking light fitting. (left)

Game, Set, (Mis)Match

Inspired by the graphic appeal of African waxed cloth? Then now is the time to update your table linen. Opt for an eclectic mix of these traditional batik-print fabrics in the form of reusable placemats and napkins, and the table is set for an anti-minimalist celebration.

An eclectic selection of utilitarian objects and a pattern-filled table surface make for a colorful dining experience. The carefully curated selection here combines ceramic and woven items, colorful placemats, and chunky recycled glass tumblers juxtaposed with a beautiful Italian-inspired contemporary blown glass jug. (below)

Electric Dreams

African textiles – in both their colors and patterns – are hardly shy or retiring, which is why they always work best against a simple, neutral backdrop. As with any successful bedroom scheme, this look (opposite) relies on layering: a characterful combination of high and low elements such as the bespoke upholstered bed frame and luxurious linen with the playful graphic cushions and tribal surface pattern of the statement turquoise basket, used here for a delicious monstera plant.

Ubiquitously African, plastic mats are the ultimate union of form, function and decoration. This sunny yellow example (right) cheerfully intervenes in an otherwise minimalist bathroom – a reminder to be less predictable and more playful when dressing up our homes.

The New Bohemian

Move over Moroccan design, sayonara sakura blossoms, and catch you later, Scandi illustrations. Open your mind – and spaces – to the inspiring and varied surface patterns of the African continent and discover their colorful, transformative appeal.

- Upholstered bed frame and bedding from Weylandts (weylandts.co.za)
- Basket (used as planter) and Shoppers (on floor), from Africa Nova
- On bed cushions made up in selection of fabrics, from Mnandi Texiles & Design (Facebook / Mnandi Textiles. Also see Vlisco (vlisco.com))
- Throw, from @ Home (home.co.za)
- Natural/blue pendant shade (behind bed frame), from Ashanti Design (ashantidesign.com)
- Woven plastic mat, from Design Afrika (designafrika.co.za)
- White stool/table, from Chair Crazy (chaircrazy.co.za)
- Kikois (just seen), from Africa Nova (Facebook / Africa Nova)
- African wax cloth fabrics (made into tea towels), from Mnandi Texiles & Design
- Assortment of vessels (just seen) on shelf and kitchen counter: Milano Bouquet Green/Transparent Vase by Ichendorf, from Guild (theguildgroup.co.za / ichendorfmilano.com)
- Zig-zag river reed woven utility baskets, Design Afrika (designafrika.co.za)
- Blue telephone wire bowl with lid, from Africa Nova (Facebook / Africa Nova)

The feeling of sonder is the realization that each individual person you pass by or see has their own complex life as unique as your own, filled with traditions, worries, emotions, and relationships.

Whether or not you are aware of another person's full life, they continually are living it all the time. They do not only exist in the moment that you are thinking of them or noticing them.

empathy & AWARENESS

sonder

All humans on this earth simultaneously each have a multi-faceted existence, filled with complications of which we are completely unaware. Each person has his/her own family, work, goals, passions, daily frets, and thoughts.

This awareness of each person's full and separate experience of life can be overwhelming, especially when you select a particular stranger that you know nothing about. But it's a beautiful reflection on empathy to consider the impact of sonder as you go about your life and interact with individual people.

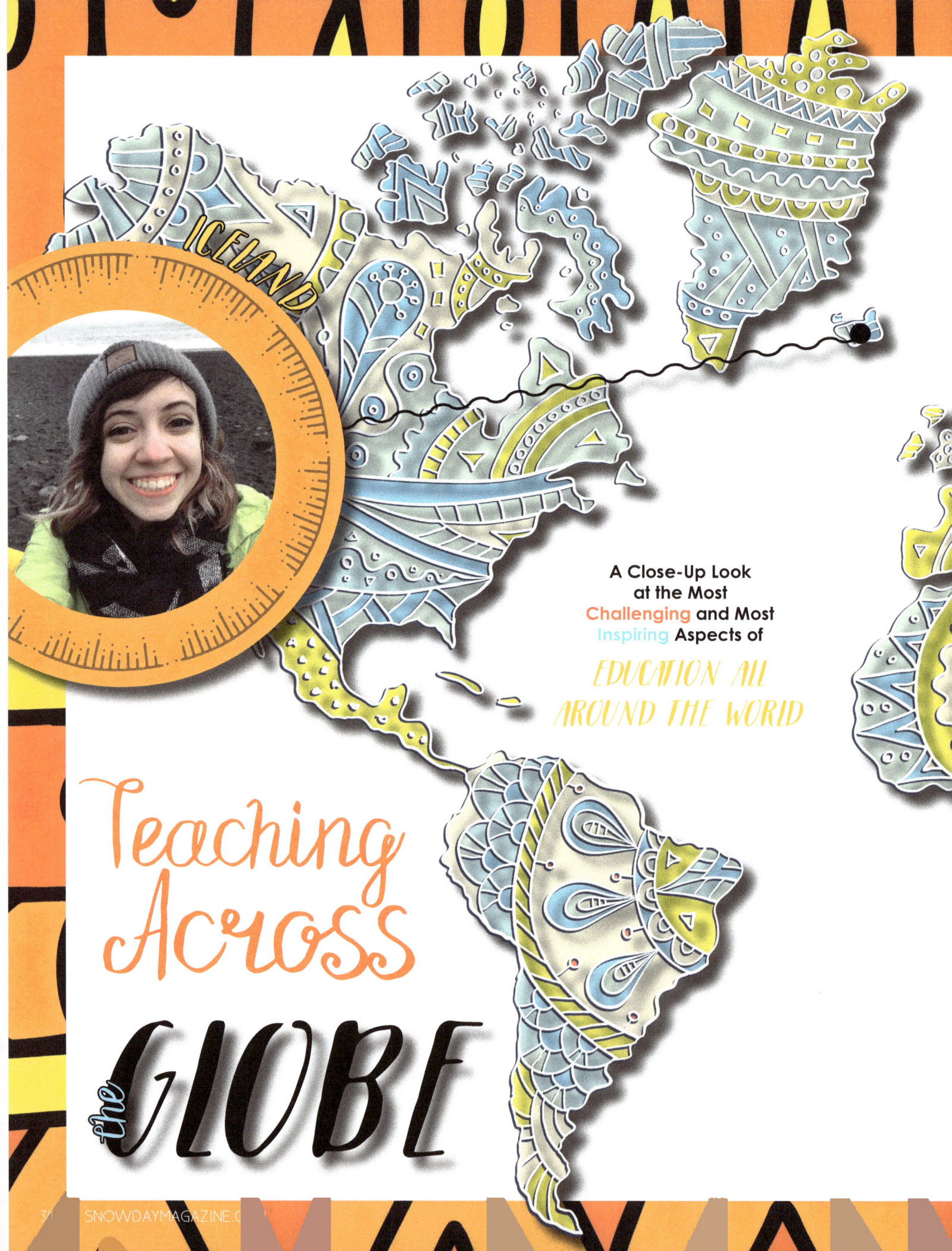

ICELAND

A Close-Up Look at the Most **Challenging** and Most **Inspiring** Aspects of

EDUCATION ALL AROUND THE WORLD

Teaching Across the GLOBE

What's Challenging in Germany:
The school district I teach in is diverse in every way you could imagine. One of the biggest challenges, therefore, is the heterogeneity of my students. The creation of differential lessons to meet the needs of every child is being challenged by a lack of professional staff, old media equipment, and additional duties for teachers. Teaching children with different educational needs in one classroom requires well educated teaching teams including a special needs teacher and enough time to prepare and organize lessons. Having to focus on a variety of additional tasks (such as managing the school's computers) can even shift the teacher's focus away from the child and towards school administration and management.

What's Challenging in England:
As with any area in education, there are challenges and obstacles that arise along the way, requiring us to think strategically and creatively about how we approach teaching and learning, in order to ensure that we maximise pupil progress. For me, one of the biggest challenges faced is the amount of content that needs to be taught each year, compared to the amount of time available. How do we push for depth and enable enough time for children to master and consolidate their learning, whilst also juggling a full curriculum? The British National curriculum is packed with a range of objectives that need to be taught within each year. Some pupils, however, may be missing the fundamental skills, foundations, or previous years' knowledge, meaning time for revisitation and practice needs to be regularly embedded within the curriculum in order to build upon this. This is a vital component if these children are to be successful moving forward. It does, however, mean that time is limited and new learning needs to be planned for efficiently to ensure that all can be covered. This is something that can be challenging.

What's Inspiring About Education in England:
One of the things I love most about working as a teacher in the United Kingdom is the plethora of opportunities given for continuous professional development. If we are to be the very best educators that we can be for the pupils that we teach, it's important that we as professionals continue to seek opportunities to better our understanding of teaching and learning. From courses to lesson studies, national qualifications to triads (creating a group of 3 with other stakeholders and working to better each other), and working alongside partner schools, there are many avenues offered to continue to develop your practise and learn from a range of educators. I'm always keen to find out more, try out ideas, and refine my understanding of the most effective pedagogy.

What's Challenging in Croatia:
Despite numerous reforms and strategies, Croatia has not escaped the global problem of social crisis. Problems that happen in society are also transferred to school desks. The crisis of values, solidarity, and empathy, as well as the general lack of interest in quality education are problems that need to be addressed urgently. For many years, there has been a controversy in educational circles on how to adapt and enrich teaching with universal values, taking into account the specifics of children of the new age. Today's students are digital natives who care about the speed and availability of information and who do not accept the classic way of teaching. The question arises at all levels of how to deal with change and how to adapt to children who have different skills, preferences, and ways of learning. All questions and controversies on this topic were interrupted this spring by the Covid crisis and the devastating earthquake that hit Zagreb. There are problems of lack of space due to the large number of earthquake-damaged schools, as well as due to strict epidemiological frameworks. All the difficulties that have befallen us can really seem like a chance to return to universal human values, solidarity, and faith in education. In the times of crisis, that is all we have left.

What's Inspiring About Education in Germany:
Ironically, I also love the diversity and heterogeneity of my school district. My classroom is as mixed as society itself and it is beautiful to see how the whole school community benefits from the different social, cultural, and ethnical backgrounds. The students grow up in an environment that needs to be based on respect and tolerance, which makes heterogeneity natural. It creates a space of cultural dialogue and leads to appreciation of diversity. I have seen students, as well as teachers and parents, grow away from prejudice in this environment and this fills my heart with happiness. The positive experience the children have is a foundation for respect, responsibility, and openmindedness. Over the last couple of years, Germany started becoming more comfortable with the influence immigration has on its society. I am very proud to be a teacher, helping my students become a part of our diverse future.

GERMANY

Anna Lena Lutz
@colorful_classroom
Stuttgart, Germany
3rd grade

Danielle
@miss_syrupbow
England, UK
Year 4 (Ages 8-9)

ENGLAND

CROATIA

Daria Stejskal
Zagreb, Croatia
7th and 8th grade

What's Inspiring About Education in Croatia:
Croatia, as a member of the European Union, is a beneficiary of the Erasmus program. In 2020, my school received a new Erasmus + KA1 project "Equal in Diversity." Nine teachers travel across Europe and attend high-value training in mindfulness, teaching games, psychosocial support for students with special needs, inclusion, innovative teaching approaches, and the development of critical thinking. Teachers travel and learn about examples of good practice across Europe. New friendships are formed, new projects are created, and horizons are expanded. What I consider particularly important in the educational process, both in Croatia and globally, is the empowerment of teachers and constant investment in education. We must not forget that the satisfaction and motivation of teachers is the basis of education.

CHINA

Erin Vaeth
@erlyva
Beijing, China
Kindergarten

Puti Almirsha
@missputialmirsha
Jakarta, Indonesia
Grade 7 to 11

INDONESIA

What's Challenging in Indonesia:
The educational system in Indonesia went through a few changes, from the conservative thematic integrated curriculum to a more competencies-based curriculum. With the new ministry of education, we are looking to a more progressive curriculum. However, the wide spread of islands in Indonesia makes it challenging to have an equal quality of curriculum across the nation. Fortunately, a few groups and communities of teachers and educators are starting the grassroots movement to widen the importance of progressive education in Indonesia.

INDIA

Saumya Pandey
@wandererexplorer
Bangalore, India
Grades 5, 6, & 7

What's Challenging in China:
Education in Beijing is extremely competitive, and there is a large emphasis placed on tests, particularly entrance tests for secondary schools and universities. This system has lead both schools and parents to put a high level of pressure on students. Starting as young as two or three years old, students will be in school from 8:30 am until 5 pm five days a week, and most students still take multiple classes outside of this timeframe! Kindergarten students usually have classes seven days a week, and complain that even the "fun" classes are not fun because they have no time to relax.

What's Inspiring About Education in China:
Many international schools in Beijing have a diverse and motivated group of students and teachers from around the world. It's really rewarding to learn from teachers who have previously been teaching in other countries, and my students were always interested in learning about new cultures. Teaching is a highly respected profession in China. Teachers at international schools are well compensated, and receive excellent benefits.

China

What's Challenging in India:
Since India is a subcontinent and a country where more than 300 languages are spoken, all of the influences, accents, and ways of life change every few miles. The biggest challenge, I personally believe, is to develop a curriculum that encompasses the ethnic diversity. Using a native language which is understood by people of a particular area also helps. Children come from a variety of backgrounds. India provides free and compulsory education until the age of 14 for all children. However, many children are forced to work and miss out on school. Creating a system that is available to everyone equally, irrespective of race, religion, social status, caste, ethnicity, and colour still remains the biggest challenge in rural areas.

What's Inspiring About Education in India:
I teach at a school which follows something called the 3C curriculum. We very much concentrate on developing character and competence in the children using a mixture of traditional Indian CBSE along with the IB curriculum. The best part about it is much of the learning is done in the form of activities outside the classroom. Teachers have the autonomy to develop and carry on their lessons their way. In my classroom most of the time we work as a team. The idea that the teacher is the finished product and can impose upon students isn't welcome in my classroom. We are just facilitators of knowledge and our primary role is facilitating pre-existing knowledge, bringing out the best, and making the kids aware of the capabilities and inbound potential they have within. In this process of being a facilitator, you end up learning more and becoming a student all over again. Without this, true learning remains incomplete.

India

What's Inspiring About Education in Indonesia:
I live in Jakarta, and teach in Jakarta and Serpong (the rural part of Jakarta) for a private owned progressive school named Sekolah Cikal (Cikal School). Cikal is a progressive, national school that aims to be the frontier of taking education to a progressive level in Indonesia. We fortunately have a great relationship with the ministry, which resulted in a lot of our educators being active in communities to help build awareness and develop other teachers professionally. We often try new approaches to teaching and learning, and new approaches in educational leadership and school management to make sure that we are innovating or finding effective strategies to improve the education system for the benefit of the students. What's great about Cikal is the faith they put in young and emerging school leaders and teachers. Our drive and ambition allow us to make mistakes and grow in our own pace and way.

Indonesia

GHANA

Madina Adutwumwaa Asare
@teacher_ewuraama
Diamond State Academy
(Kumasi-Ghana)
Grade 1 (6 to 7 years)

What's Challenging in Ghana:
Some of the schools are lacking computers for practicals and research. Due to this, teaching is difficult for most of the teachers in my area. Some students also lack educational materials like stationeries, exercise books, writing tools, reading books, dictionaries, pencils, etc. Most students lack chairs due to the number of students in one class. Some of the students sit on the floor to learn.

Some students find it difficult to bring food to eat when they are in school so they wait for the school food that is lunch. Most students eat once a day (when they are in school) due to financial problems in their homes. Lack of drinking water is another one of the biggest challenges we face in my area.

What's Inspiring About Education in Ghana:
Our great teachers make learning fun, as stimulating, engaging lessons are pivotal to a student's academic success. Some students who are more prone to misbehaviour, truancy, or disengagement are more dependent on an engaging teacher. Making your classroom an exciting environment for learning holds the students' fascination, and students learn best when they are both challenged and interested. It's part of motivating students, which may not be easy, but which will benefit students immeasurably in the long run.

The inspiring educator strives to spark motivation in all students in a way that spurs academic achievement and galvanizes success via motivational influence.

As a teacher, have you been inspired to work harder or pursue a particular goal? Were you inspired to become an educator by one of your own great teachers? Inspiration can take many forms, from helping a pupil through the academic year and their short-term goals, to guiding them towards their future career. Years after graduation, many working professionals will still cite a particular teacher as the one who fostered their love of what they currently do and attribute their accomplishments to that educator.

NIGERIA

Okoye Jecinta
@thelovefilledteacher
Nigeria in Rivers State
Kindergarten 2
& High School

What's Challenging in Nigeria:
1. We have a lack of instructional or teaching materials.
2. There is a refusal to employ teachers to teach all the subjects required by the school in order to help relieve some teachers who are made to teach more than one subject. This happens simply because the school owners try to manage funds or school fees paid and make the teachers suffer and stress themselves. Because of this, the teachers are underpaid after teaching sometimes three different subjects from Year 1 to Year 5 while only getting paid for one subject.

What's Inspiring About Education in Ghana:
We are not expected to spend all our day at school. We get to close for work early enough to go do other things we would love to do.

SOUTH AFRICA

Yasira
@mrs_optimus_primary
Vanderbijlpark,
South Africa
Grades 4-6 (Ages 8-12)

What's Challenging in South Africa:
South Africa is a third world country. The problem with our education system comes from the top down. The leaders in the education sector are not well educated themselves and are not aware of how to properly manage the education in our country. Teachers are underpaid and classrooms have to accommodate up to 75 learners. This is because money that needs to be spent on building schools is going into the pockets of the current leadership. Our teachers are treated very poorly and as much as they try, they're getting tired and frustrated. Many principals in the public school sector are taking bribes. Teachers who have now lost their passion and motivation are not delivering the best work they should be. We are also a country that's been a democratic nation for only 26 years. The past is still creeping up on us with half of our people coming from disadvantaged homes where the department of education has to lower the standards of education and pass rate to accommodate a problem that should've been fixed years ago. In a nutshell, we deal with corruption within our education sector, uneducated leaders, schools being overfilled with learners, underpaid teachers, lower pass rates, and a very low standard of education that doesn't always cater to every child. Learners with special needs are left in classrooms that don't cater to them, as parents can't always afford private schooling for them.

What's Inspiring About Education in South Africa:
As a country, no matter how difficult our situation is or how unmotivated we feel, we always get through it together. South Africans have developed a way to handle our issues and it's across all sectors. We use our humour and warm spirit to tackle problems. We persevere. As teachers, fellow teachers may know, we have an immense amount of patience. No matter how hard teachers are knocked down, we get up and we try harder. We have qualified teachers working for a minimum wage and they still pull through doing the best they can.

What's Challenging in Fiji:
We have big class sizes (40 children per teacher). Teachers have to fork out from their pockets to buy school supplies. Too much paper work must be done by teachers. This leaves less time to spend on contact hours and planning.

What's Challenging in New Zealand:
Mental health is a big issue in New Zealand and neither teachers nor students are immune to this. Unfortunately, youth suicide, child abuse, and poverty rates are some of the highest in the world here. Teachers are at the coalface of this epidemic and are very under resourced. We'd love to see more counselors in schools and funding for students to get the help they need from a younger age.

What's Inspiring About Education in New Zealand:
Teaching in New Zealand is great as our curriculum is very open ended and flexible, meaning there is room for all sorts of exciting learning and every classroom and teacher offers something unique based on their own interests and those of their learners.

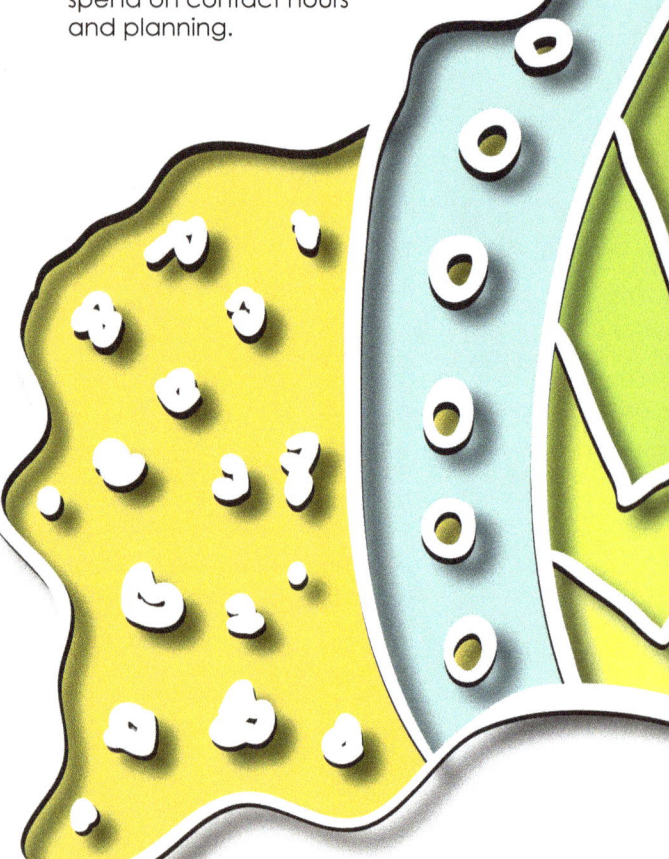

Current trends include play based learning for younger students and developing older learners' ability to self assess and find their own strengths and next learning steps.

Students are taught at their own level and pace and we try to keep assessment minimal. There is certainly no passing or failing at the primary level. We also don't have specialist teachers, meaning we get to enjoy all the subjects of the curriculum with our kids and every day is different.

FIJI

Ruci Tukana
@ms_tukana
Suva, Fiji
English Language and Literature
Grades 8, 9 and 10

What's Inspiring About Education in Fiji:
As an English Access Microscholarship Program Instructor, I would say I am unique from the rest of my colleagues because I teach the American Syllabus. What is great about teaching where I live is that my country is multiracial. We have the Native Fijians, Indians, Chinese, Rotumans, Phillipinos, and white children (children of expats and diplomats). We also have some Nigerians and heaps of Pacific Islanders like Papua New Guineans, Gilbertese, Naurusns, Samoans, Tongans, Solmon Islanders, etc. We teach cultural diversity as well.

NEW ZEALAND

Rosie
@teachcreate
Auckland, New Zealand
Years 3 and 4 (Ages 7-9)

New Zealand

What's Challenging in Canada:
There are a number of challenges within our educational system. One challenge that particularly hits close to home is the lack of support for children's mental health and social emotional well-being. Students need an abundance of mental health services, but schools don't have enough resources to meet the demand. Services are failing to catch up, and in the meantime, students are left in the dark.

CANADA

Mariette Xerri
@lovelivelaughteach
Mississauga, Canada
Grades 7 and 8
Special Education

What's Challenging in Canada (continued):
Furthermore, with our current pandemic, support for mental health should be at the forefront of all students' learning, yet lack of funding and programs continues in our area. Our students need the strong supports in place to help them navigate their big feelings in our world, develop positive coping strategies, and build confidence that they are capable and able beings. Building connection and establishing positive relationships with our students can set the foundation for social, emotional, mental, and academic well being.

What's Inspiring About Education in Canada:
As our nation continues to grow, the one aspect that sets us apart from other countries is that we have the privilege of teaching in culturally diverse classrooms. Children in our classrooms come from so many different backgrounds, cultures, and races. Celebrating and valuing diversity in our classrooms is part of our daily classroom life. Teaching children to be proud of themselves and their family traditions and the importance of respecting and valuing people regardless of the colour of their skin, their physical abilities, or the language they speak is all part of the diverse classroom culture we share in Canada. Being educated in a culturally diverse classroom also supports learners to become critical thinkers about race, prejudice, stereotypes, and discrimination. As teachers in Canada continue to engage children from all over the world, we openly learn about identity and help foster a positive sense of self in children. This helps children build bridges across cultures and traditions while supporting our culturally diverse schools. The more that children have a solid foundation and understanding about who they are and where they came from, the more they confidently grow with a strong sense of self and the closer we come to building a world of mutual respect and acceptance.

What's Challenging in Costa Rica:
Right now we have to be very careful with the kids about using masks. We have to do different activities where physical contact does not exist in order to be able to have a healthy environment. Sometimes having to be right behind the students to make sure they follow hygiene protocols gets tiring, but we are happy to see the kids happy around the school.

What's Inspiring About Education in Costa Rica:
We try to challenge the students to go beyond their comfort zone so they can learn to achieve a goal. It requires perseverance and a positive mindset. These are skills that they can transfer to their personal lives, and apply to their relationships with family and community members. In my prospective career as an educator at this institution, I look forward to working in a collaborative learning and teaching environment with both teachers and students.

Paola Alvarado Freer
@PaoFreer
Guanacaste, Costa Rica
Pk to 10th

COSTA RICA

What's Challenging in Brazil:
Insufficient training for teachers prevents some of our teachers from understanding the importance of applying current methods and best practices in public schools. Public schools located in peripheral regions are not well integrated, which makes it hard for them to collaborate with their community.

What's Inspiring About Education in Brazil:
We have a rich awareness of the social, historical, and cultural identity of our territories.

What's Challenging in Argentina:
The educational system in Argentina is facing hard times. My country's public school system used to be one of the best in Latin America but under-investment has led to its decline. Economic crisis has promoted budget cuts that replicated and reinforced social inequality. Thus, teachers are forced to tackle situations where students are facing domestic violence, broken families, drugs, and hunger. Public schools are not all equipped with updated resources (such as technology and classroom equipment). Nonetheless, our teachers are the ones who have the challenge to do our best to improve this. I have always been inspired by the passion of teaching to promote learning in an enjoyable and engaging way. I work to establish strong bonds among my students.

Brazil

Argentina

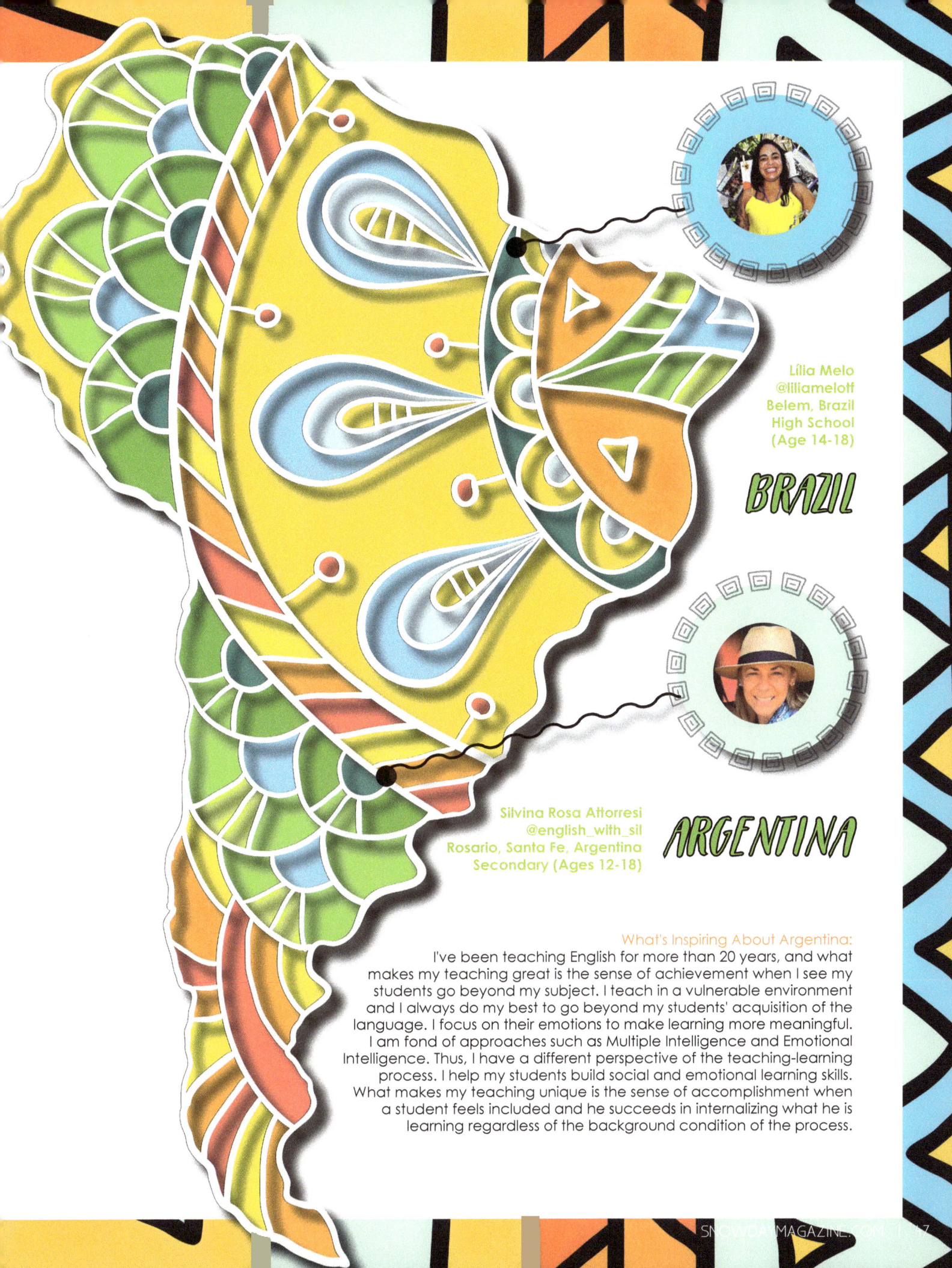

Lília Melo
@liliamelotf
Belem, Brazil
High School
(Age 14-18)

BRAZIL

Silvina Rosa Attorresi
@english_with_sil
Rosario, Santa Fe, Argentina
Secondary (Ages 12-18)

ARGENTINA

What's Inspiring About Argentina:
I've been teaching English for more than 20 years, and what makes my teaching great is the sense of achievement when I see my students go beyond my subject. I teach in a vulnerable environment and I always do my best to go beyond my students' acquisition of the language. I focus on their emotions to make learning more meaningful. I am fond of approaches such as Multiple Intelligence and Emotional Intelligence. Thus, I have a different perspective of the teaching-learning process. I help my students build social and emotional learning skills. What makes my teaching unique is the sense of accomplishment when a student feels included and he succeeds in internalizing what he is learning regardless of the background condition of the process.

Greek philosophers developed the term "acatalepsy" to describe the impossibility of ever fully comprehending the universe.

We can never fully grasp the endless beauty, diversity, and vast expanses of the earth. Although we can understand certain aspects of science and reflect in awe on the many marvels of this world, our minds will always be searching for truth. When we are at a loss to explain or comprehend our universe, we must be content to sit in wonder.

acatalepsy

vast & INCOMPREHENSIBLE

@TASSELAMOR

The Tassel Amor shop sells beautifully colored vibrant tassels, poms, and earrings handcrafted by women in Mexico. The merchandise is stunning and would make a perfect, unique gift!

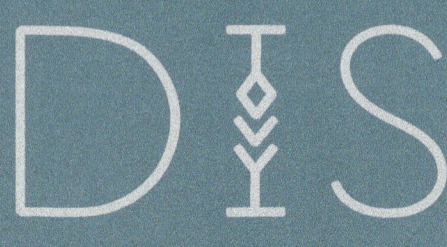

DIYS

@TEGATEA

Tega provides award-winning and Fair Trade certified tea. They aim to close the gender gap and to extend the benefits of fair trade to more women and girls. Not only are Tega teas delicious and healthy, but they are improving the lives of workers in countries marginalized by trade.

@ELEGANTEES

Elegantees is on a mission to fight human trafficking in Nepal through job creation for survivors and those at risk. They are so much more than stylish clothing; they are motivated to use sewing as a means to restore lives and maintain independent living.

@MOYAASHEABUTTER

Moyaa Shea Butter improves your skin while improving the world around us. They are based in Canada and use Grade A Organic Shea, one of the absolute best moisturizers for the skin.

@YENISIBEAUTY

The founders of Yenisi Beauty, who love all things natural, provide ethically sourced skincare and haircare. In addition, their products are organic, vegan, and cruelty-free!

COVER

fair trade gifts

Fair trade is a global movement that puts people and the planet first. It's made up of a diverse network of producers, companies, consumers, advocates, and organizations. When you choose fair trade, you can reduce poverty, support environmentally friendly practices, and protect safe and humane working conditions. Prioritize ethical practices by following, supporting, and shopping with these stunning and affordable top picks.

@SYMBOLOGYCLOTHING

Symbology clothing is a brick and mortar store that instills confidence in women all over the world. They empower both the maker and wearer by offering unique and stylish clothing using artisanal fabric techniques. Symbology also incorporates meaningful motifs and symbols in their designs that reflect a deep heritage and can be admired as a form of cultural art.

@SWAHILIMODERN

Swahili Modern works directly with artisans all throughout Africa, who create striking handmade home decor items and other household objects. Handwoven by Senegalese women, their collection of baskets and hampers would be a unique addition to anyone's home.

@SHOPGYPSYFREEDOM

Gypsy Freedom merges style and awareness while making ethical shopping accessible to the everyday woman. Their clothes are both trendy and relaxed. Follow the shop to become a more conscious shopper!

@DARZAHDESIGNS

Darzah showcases beautiful hand-embroidered shoes and bags handcrafted in Palestine. They specialize in Palestinian "tatreez" embroidery, an art form that has been passed down from generation to generation for centuries. In addition to celebrating Palestinian culture, they also employ refugee and low-income women.

@SUREHOUSECOFFEE

Sure House Coffee Roasting Co. is a fair trade organic microroaster in Ohio. They roast the beans right in the back of the shop, and enjoy crafting unique drinks like a lavender honey latte.

wander THE world

Travel can offer teachers unique cultural experiences and a variety of new perspectives on life. Even educators who've already found a passion for global adventures often feel that their wanderlust cannot be satisfied. However, the perceived challenges can in fact be easily overcome or turned into opportunities. As teachers, we are actually in a unique position to be able to travel with great frequency. By taking advantage of these special opportunities for teachers, budget tips, and travel strategies, you'll be able to wander the world in a way that many other professionals would envy.

ON A TEACHER BUDGET

by Shannon of
Traveling Teacher Girl
@travelingteachergirl

Travel offers the chance to learn about other cultures and see how other people live. During my first trip to Europe, where I assumed that the lifestyle in big cities would be similar to the lifestyle here in New York City, I noticed huge differences in how people live. For example, in many European cities, a much larger emphasis is placed on reusing, recycling, and being less wasteful with our planet's limited resources. Living an eco-friendly lifestyle has always been very important to me, and witnessing how people live in other countries made me realize just how much further I needed to go in order to be less wasteful.

The same shift in perspective happens even when traveling to different areas in the United States. I live in a huge city, so my priorities and experiences might be different than someone who lives in a very rural environment. Seeing these differences allows you to be more empathetic and understanding of other people's priorities and ways of thinking.

In addition to being a more understanding and globally-conscious citizen, this awareness also spreads into the classroom to make you a better teacher. Our students often come from different backgrounds, cultures, and home environments than us, and it is important to be aware of this. This perspective helps when teaching in the classroom, and it also helps when communicating with students' families.

I teach pre-k music at a public school in Brooklyn. (Yes- teaching pre-k music can actually be a full time job. I feel super lucky to have such a unique and fun position.) In addition, I have a private studio of flute, guitar, and piano students.

I did my first big international trip somewhat recently, in 2015, after my first year of teaching. I had the desire to travel for a long time before that and always wanted to study or teach abroad when I was in college, but I was always worried about the cost of these programs or having to add extra semesters in school so I never went for it. However, after my first year of teaching I realized how lucky I was to have a schedule with so many weeks off, so I scheduled my first big trip. During this trip I visited 6 different countries in Europe over the course of three weeks, and I was totally bit by the travel bug. I was blown away by the amount of beauty in the world, and was also amazed by how affordable travel can be if you are really strategic with your planning. Since then, I have visited over 20 countries and have travelled during almost every summer vacation and school break.

culture

Loving Snowday? Snap a pic and share on social.

travel
ON A BUDGET

In general, there are two things that hold people back from traveling more: having time off of work, and being able to afford it. Most teachers on a traditional schedule already have the first part covered. This is a major luxury, especially here in the United States, where unfortunately, most jobs do not provide much vacation time.

So, the next step is figuring out the budget side of things. There are two major parts of my life that help me to afford travel: having a side hustle so I can maximize my income, and knowing how to book affordable trips.

First, I will talk a bit about possible side hustles and maximizing your income. If your school offers you salary raises for credits earned beyond your undergraduate or graduate degrees, I recommend doing this ASAP. The cost of taking these classes is only going to increase with time, so it is in your best interest to get them done as soon as you can. In addition, the sooner you move up the salary scale, the more years you will have to enjoy the extra income. Many schools offer a $4,000-$10,000 salary boost when you complete extra credits, which means earning an additional $40,000-$100,000 in just the first ten years after completing these credits. This is huge. Don't underestimate how quickly that adds up. If your school offers salary raises for additional credits, get those courses done ASAP.

Another way to earn additional income is to have a side hustle. In addition, there are many ways to set up a passive income stream as a teacher. These require a bit of a time investment at first, but can be a nice source of passive income once they are established.

BEST SIDE-HUSTLES FOR TEACHERS

>> Babysit
>> Tutor (in person or online)
>> Teach online
>> House sit or pet sit
>> Become a virtual assistant
>> Offer services on TaskRabbit
>> Write as a freelancer

PASSIVE INCOME OPTIONS

>> Sell curriculum or materials on TeachersPayTeachers
>> Start an education blog and earn money through ads on your site and / or affiliate marketing
>> Create an online course and sell it on an online platform such as Udemy
>> Share your knowledge through Youtube or Podcasts (However, be aware that you need more than 1,000 subscribers on Youtube to earn money through ads.)
>> Create/sell an eBook

Next, it is important to plan and book your vacations in a way that will stretch your vacation dollars and allow you to travel as often as possible. Here are a few tips:

8 TIPS FOR BUDGET TRAVEL:

1. In general, book as far as possible in advance for the best prices
2. Be flexible with your travel dates to get the best prices (This is easiest during summer vacation.)
3. Track prices on GoogleFlights to book at the cheapest moment
4. Be flexible with your destination (Ex: try searching for broad regions such as Caribbean or Europe in GoogleFlights rather than specific cities)
5. Research accommodations at hotels, airbnbs, and hostels. The cheapest option often varies by city.
6. Look for package deals on TravelZoo, Groupon, and CheapCaribbean.
7. Avoid eating/drinking at tourist spots – Ask locals for recommendations, or picnic outdoors
8. Pack light to save money on checked bags

In addition, be sure to take advantage of credit card points. A few of my favorites are the Barclay Arrival Card and Capital One Venture Card, which offer between 50,000 and 70,000 bonus miles after opening your account and spending a certain amount. This amounts to about $500-$700 cash back.

In addition to traditional travel and vacations, teachers have some free travel options available if you are interested in teaching, working, or researching abroad. There are a variety of government organizations, private companies, and non-profit international organizations who sponsor travel grants specifically for teachers. These grants are perfect for teachers who want to broaden their horizons and improve their teaching practice abroad. These programs all differ in requirements and details, but in general, they are highly competitive and involve some type of research or teaching while abroad. They can vary in length from one week to one year. Check out my blog for a list of over 30 fellowship and grant programs that offer free travel to teachers.

My own most disappointing travel experience was horseback riding in the ocean in Jamaica. I was staying at a nice resort and decided to book this excursion through the resort last minute as I was checking in. I had seen many photos of people horseback riding in the ocean, and I thought that it would be a magical experience. However, when I arrived at the tour, I saw that the horses were underfed, malnourished, and very poorly trained. The tour guide was rough with the horses and was only able to lead them through intimidation.

When we got to the ocean, the tour guide led us into the water one at a time with our horses. However, the horses were terrified of the water and were struggling to swim with people on their backs, grunting and moaning as they kept their heads above the deep water. After seeing the first few people go into the water, the majority of our tour group decided to not go in the water with our horses because we felt so bad for these poor animals. This experience still haunts me, and I regret booking this excursion and putting my tourist dollars towards an inhumane company. While my experience happened in Jamaica, this experience could have happened anywhere and is a cautionary tale to always do your research before booking activities, especially when they involve animals.

On a more positive note, one of my favorite parts of traveling is eating! If I have the time, I try to research restaurants ahead of time that I would like to visit. Most countries use TripAdvisor to rate restaurants, so I usually start there. In addition, ask your hotel or Airbnb host for

recommendations- they usually know the best spots that aren't tourist traps.

In addition to eating at restaurants, I try to picnic as much as possible to save some money and also to explore/enjoy the outdoors. One of my favorite travel memories is sitting along the Seine in Paris with a picnic lunch and champagne. It is also really fun to explore local grocery stores and see the different options that they have. I love seeing the weird snacks that other countries have compared to the snacks we have in the U.S. (that I am sure look equally as weird to people who aren't from the U.S.)

>> travelingteachergirl.com

8 Photography Tips When Traveling

>> Arrive at popular spots early to beat the crowds (and to also get that beautiful morning light!)
>> Have patience- If you are at a crowded spot, wait a few minutes for it to clear out for your perfect shot.
>> Be confident- Don't worry if people are watching you while you take a photo.
>> Add movement! This brings more energy to photos and makes them look more natural. Some easy ideas include walking towards the camera, looking around at the sites, and chatting/laughing with the person taking your photo.
>> Plan outfits that are photogenic. Flowy skirts are super comfortable for traveling and also look great in photos!
>> If you are traveling solo and need help getting a photograph, offer to take a photo for a nearby person or group. They will usually be happy to take a photo for you in return.
>> Crop/edit your photos to bring them to life. I use the app Adobe Lightroom for this.
>> Experiment with different angles. Sometimes holding the camera a little lower or a little higher can totally transform a photo.

5 Reasons Teachers Should Travel More

1. To deepen your understanding of other cultures
2. To learn about the world around you and then bring that knowledge to your classroom
3. To have a chance to focus on yourself and your own needs rather than the needs of others
4. Because having time off of work is a luxury that we should take advantage of!
5. Because teaching is HARD and all teachers deserve the chance to refuel and re-energize

words and images by
Vienna Rose
@viennaroseco

how to

CREATE a COZY HOME

One of the best parts of adventuring around the globe is coming back to your home base. Having a beautiful and cozy home to return to can bring great comfort, and dreaming up the perfect combination of layers of textures in a moodboard is half the fun! Here are 9 tips for making your own home a refuge that recharges you and nourishes your soul.

You walk up your driveway after a long, but fulfilling day at work, turn the key and open the door... What greets you?

Do you see a space that gives you joy? Or do you feel overwhelmed and indifferent?

Creating a cozy home and a space that makes you feel happy and comfortable is so important. Considering that we have spent most of this year at home, and will continue to do so in other seasons, it's time to invest in your home.

simple, textured, & tidy

relaxation

1. SEASONAL CLEANING

Spring cleaning doesn't just have to happen in spring! Sorting and culling items in your home is a great way to reorganize, tidy and simplify. Trust me, when you finally tackle that cupboard harbouring all those items you've been avoiding, you are going to feel amazing.

In 2018, I moved from New Zealand to Norway. I had to recreate my new apartment into a space that made me feel at home in a foreign country. Even after two years, I'm still looking for new ways to make it even more cozy (call me obsessed). You don't need thousands of dollars to improve your home, but with some simple tips and careful spending, you too can create a place that soothes your soul.

What steps can you take to create a cozy home that raises your spirits and recharges you? Here are nine tips to get you on your way to your new and improved space.

EYE CATCHING ENTRY

Have a statement piece that is in your line of sight as soon as you open your door. Whether it's a piece of art, a vase of colorful flowers, or a shelf styled with some of your favorite trinkets, make sure it's something that lights you up as you step inside.

CANDLES

You can never have too many candles! A Norwegian friend of mine used to have at least 30 candles burning during the midst of winter. This was the norm for her! The warm glow of flickering light in the dark really helped to create a relaxed and cozy environment.

TEXTURES

Having a variety of textures in a space will create a rich scheme full of depth. Instead of choosing just one texture and replicating it, try different materials and thicknesses, layering them on each other. Do you own a couple of rugs made from different materials? Try placing the smallest on top of the biggest for a different look. To redress your sofa for the colder months, opt for accessories such as cushion covers in heavier fabrics like velvet or blankets in faux fur.

4

texture

blend natural light and ambient light

6

AMBIENT LIGHT

In addition to candles, there are other forms of mood lighting you can add to your home. Turn off your harsh ceiling lights and instead use fairy lights, floor lamps, table lamps or wall sconces with dimmed or soft, warm light.

STATEMENT PIECE

Every room needs a statement piece. It's like the star of the show, the piece that first draws your eye while the other items support it. Maybe it's a large mirror, craft piece or framed picture. Whatever it is, make sure other pieces aren't competing with it for attention.

5

If you are trying to make a small space seem bigger, try to find furniture with legs that sit off the floor. This makes sure light isn't constricted and travels through the space, and gives the illusion of a bigger room.

7 LISTS

Chances are, you are going to want one of everything. Sadly, this is not possible for most of us unless we can chuck it on a credit card and not think about it. A savvy way of collecting all the pieces you have your eye on is to write a list of items you want and prioritze them. Number them from 1-5 and so on to get an idea of what you want the most and tick the items off as you go.

For more interior styling, see @viennarose.co on Instagram

curation

Second hand finds are the best! You can always find a bargain. I am in love with my peacock chair. I've wanted one for years and this is the perfect size for our apartment.

MOOD BOARDS

One of my favorite ways to visualize a new scheme is to use a program like stylesourcebook.com.au This website is a tool for making your own moodboard, a digital collection of decor and furnishings for a scheme. Here you can upload pictures of items you want and pair them with matching pieces. You can also click and drag items from the website's partner retailers. This is a great way to see what your space will look like before you purchase anything!

BARGAIN HUNT

I firmly believe you don't have to pay full price for anything. Sign up for newsletter discounts, shop around to find a better price, and keep an eye out for sales. There's always a smarter way to get what you want.

By implementing these tips in the next few weeks or months, you will finally have that moment when you get home from a long but fulfilling day, open the front door, turn the key, and say...

"ahh, my cozy home!"

Although the term "sisu" originated in Finland, the concept spreads across the globe. Cultures all around the world value integrity and honor.

The word means something similar to "stoic tenacity," and includes characteristics of determination and resilience, but the understood definition within the Finnish culture goes a level deeper than that. It's more than just having grit or persevering toward a goal. It embodies an almost mystical force that is at work throughout an entire lifetime. To have a philosophy of sisu is to convert challenges into intentionality, leading to a shift in the future self.

It reflects a constant attitude of overcoming exhaustion, plowing through hard times, and forging pathways that pass directly through what you previously thought was your upper limit.

Sisu is an art of courage that must be practiced daily in order to strengthen it for when it's truly needed. It's about building the hardiness you need for when life is bound to get tough.

All across the globe, we face challenges that require standing up for our honor, persevering, and soldiering on through the daily battles.

PASSING NOTES

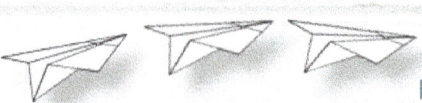

"Cultural differences should not separate us from each other, but rather cultural diversity brings a collective strength that can benefit all of humanity"
>> Robert Alan

What specific strategies help you embrace cultural diversity and teach global awareness in your classroom?

Whenever I use food examples, I use stuff some of the kids **have never heard of.** During macromolecules: hummus, carnitas tacos (carnitas is roast pork, like lechon), hot dog, pizza, chicken curry (including discussion of Indian, Thai, and Jamaican curries), fried chicken, and ice cream.

In years past I've brought in the foods for kids to try.

For cell respiration we're going to try kefir, kombucha, and sauerkraut or kimchi. A few kids are familiar with each, but none of them have had all 3. We talk about countries where these are eaten by everyone and fermented foods are common.

>> *Brittany, Science*

Basing lessons off of the Teaching Tolerance social justice standards (especially the 2nd theme of diversity) really helps me center diversity in my instruction and helps me guide kids into really constructive and enlightening conversations.

>> *Kaylee, 3rd grade*

I really enjoy teaching our unit on Christmas Around the World because we look at the globe and talk about **different countries, the people who live there and their customs.** I think it is important for children to realize the diversity in the world and to **celebrate these differences!**

>> *Virginia, Kindergarten*

I have found that the more globally aware **I become**, the better I am able to pass that awareness on to my students. Whether it is sharing my experience with impoverished schools in Tanzania, looking at racism in America, or teaching about Indigenous Tribes of Wyoming, I must **first connect with people to gain understanding**, and then move deeper into the human level of global and cultural issues.

>> *Chris, 4th grade*

To tackle the problem of social diversity (in and out of the classroom) I try to foster inclusion and acceptance. A good way to make your students feel unique is by getting to know them well. Ask them to write or design a flyer about themselves - with likes, hobbies, interests, dreams, and what makes them unique. Share them with the group and let them talk about it. This makes them feel respected by their peers.

>> *Silvina, Secondary Teacher*

Incorporate **math history**.

>> *Sharon, Math*

Use references from around the world and not just your country or culture of origin AND accompany your references with pictures/video. For example, use **jewelry making from around the world for geometric and pattern representation in geometry.**

>> *Anna, Geometry & AP Calculus AB*

An artifact always captivates. Have the children research it. Write a few sentences about it. Share within their group. Then, as a whole group, all ideas are written on chart paper and displayed throughout the teaching unit.

>> *Peggy, Retired Teacher (PK - 5)*

@imaginelilone

"We started with identifying Austria on the world map and painting the map according to its flag colours. We then did some research on the various facts of the country and read up about a famous person from Austria: Mozart.

We also used some coloured rice on cardboard to represent the Northern Limestone Alps in Austria. This allowed us to talk about how the Alps make many areas in Austria uninhabitable therefore causing it not to be too densely populated as a whole."

@miniplay2learn

To teach orienteering, try "a slightly different twist to the usual treasure hunt." The activity that this teacher-mom developed provides "a birds eye view of the garden" on each of five cards. Each one has a separate red flag to find. Each time the student or team finds one using the map that shows where it's hidden, it's time to come back for the next clue card.

Ideas to adapt this activity include blowing a whistle to show that you've found one, or customizing it for older children and their learning goals by using north, south, east, and west for indicating the location of the next clue instead of just handing it to them.

geography
IDEA HUB

When exploring geography (or even history), it's critical that students learn not only about the physical features of a particular land, but also about the daily life, climate, people, practices, and cultures.

Teaching geography more effectively can help us to share a variety of diverse perspectives that will help our students grow.

This collection of ideas will help your students to investigate the terrain and cultures of the earth, develop map skills, and explore all the different aspects of learning geography.

Talk about the beauty of each land as well as the issues, industries, political practices, wildlife, and unique landforms. These hands-on activities will guide your students to uncover the diversity of our globe.

@homeeducation.blog

"We made a map of Slovakia together. We placed the capital, big and small towns, and villages on the map. We drew the roads, the railway, and the rivers. This lesson was about helping my kids to understand what the words state, country, town, and village mean, as they were often confused when we travelled."

@goosebuddybug

When studying Geography, be sure to also investigate people and cultures. Using the book *Children Just Like Me* by Barnabas & Anabel Kindersley, students can learn about the families, clothing, homes, and foods of children all across the world. Accompany it with an art project that adds dimension with burlap or cardboard.

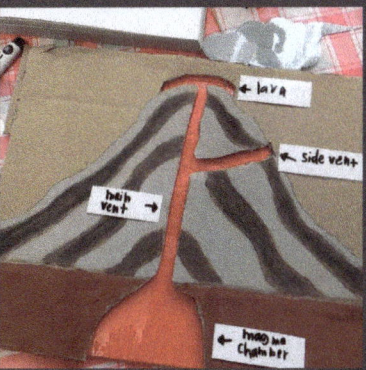

@imaginelilone

Draw a volcano on cardboard and cut out the magma chamber and vents. Tape a string behind a laminated red paper placed between the cardboard volcano and another cardboard. Glue the edges of the cardboard together so that the student can pull the string to see the magma rising.

@muddly_puddly

Avvy from The Muddly Puddly Laboratory shares, "I traced out a big world map, and watched my daughter trace it again with her fingers.

She poured sand over the deserts, scattered leaves over the forests, and placed white pebbles over the ice plains – sometimes densely, sometimes sparsely, following the coloured code on her Usborne Picture Atlas.

She brushed it all into place, and brought her animals out to live in their natural habitats, just like in her atlas. Turtles splashed into the sea and a kangaroo called out across an ocean to a giraffe in Africa.

We patted the world all over, chatting about all the countries her friends and family are from, about the languages and animals and food and temperatures and mountains and rivers and jungles and buildings and seasons, all under our careful fingers."

@thewitchisdeadhomeed

"I picked half of the town's fallen blooms last night and we used it for a great purpose. We coloured our continents with it.

We focused on terrain and weather to colour code each place and reflect it through our wild pickings."

@playplaymonkeys

Craft an entire class set of map puzzles using printables like this set from Seterra Geography.

@the_crafty_kiwi_teacher

"I used a chalkboard marker to write countries and their capitals on magnetic tiles for a little matching game. This was such a versatile activity. I might try it with languages too by matching words from other languages to English." (Inspired by @flisatfun and @resources4learning)

@danielle.s.allen

Map tracing builds familiarity and can be easily repeated by early finishers with a wipe-clean sleeve.

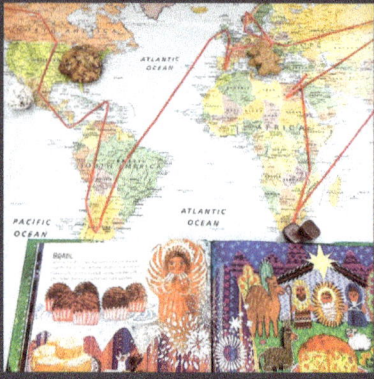

@learncraftgrow

@cirquedusewell

@schoolathomeandbeyond

"Who doesn't love the classic game of memory? These cardboard continent cards provided a fun way for the kids to learn the names of the continents and to recognize the way they look.

To make these, I cut the continents out of felt and glued them onto the cardboard cards. I then wrote out all the continent names.

HOW TO PLAY: Mix all of the cards and lay them face down. Turn over any two cards, and if they match keep them. If they don't match, turn them back over. The goal of the game is to get the most matches."

"I was inspired by the book *A World Of Cookies for Santa* by M.E. Furman and decided to do a little geography lesson along with it while munching on a variety of cookies. This book takes you around the world and talks about how different countries welcome Santa (and what name they have given him) each year.

As I read each country's information, the kids searched the map for that country and then taped our yarn down as a part of Santa's Christmas Eve route. We made a variety of cookies and discussed the different cultures while we snacked!"

"This year we're delving into a study of physical geography – namely continents, land forms, biomes, habitats, zoology, and indigenous peoples. Here's what's on our shelves:

Top shelf (from left to right): @wasecabiomes Continent Portfolios, and Continent boxes, which are filled with materials and study cards for each continent (boxes made by @treasuresfromjennifer).

Second shelf:
Montessori Map Work book, Pin Punching material for use with the Montessori world map puzzle, Montessori globe, Continents dice, Habitats book, and Continents 3-part cards.

Third shelf:
Natural World book, 3-part biome cards, Elementary Continent Game from @wasecabiomes, Cards and arrows for use with the Waseca Biomes Backyard Biome mat, The Wondrous Workings of Planet Earth book, and Cosmic Nesting boxes by @wasecabiomes.

Bottom shelf:
Landform trays, Landform cards, Landform figures and cards for use with the @wasecabiomes Landform mat, and Water + Land book.

To the right of the geography shelves, and new to our classroom this year, is our letter board. We'll use it as a gentle reminder of scripture, affirmations, and good quotes. Below the letter board are several geography books, and below those is our @spielgaben set. Finally, squeezed between the Spielgaben and geography shelves are geography mats from Waseca Biomes."

"Man cannot discover new oceans unless he has the courage to lose sight of the shore."
>> Andre Gide

@raisingshanaya

Allow students to model the different features of the Earth's surface by molding them with play dough. Having a few small tree models or animals on hand can make this even more engaging for students working in pairs.

@theorganizedhomeschool

High schoolers like hands-on learning too. After reading *Queen of Water*, one student made a cookie model of Ecuador, with the Amazon, the capital, volcanoes, and cities from the book.

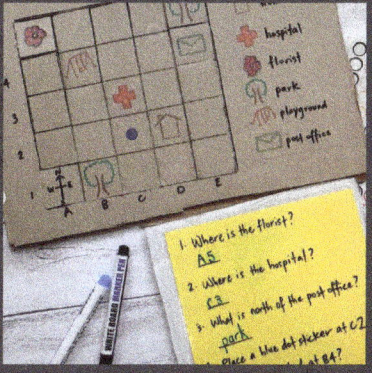

@imaginelilone

Make your map skills activities re-useable by cutting small, interchangeable squares out of carboard, or by using marker on the back of Scrabble tiles. This way, you can change up the location of each landmark every time students practice. Say "place the park at C3 and the playground southwest of it."

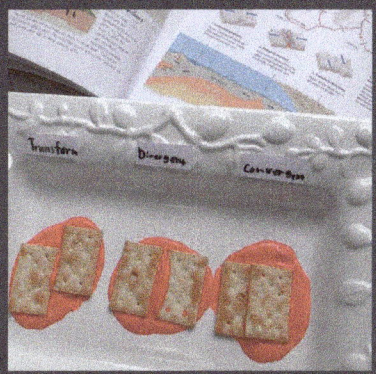

@imaginelilone

"Since we've learnt about transform plate boundaries and earthquakes a few weeks ago, I decided to introduce the other two plate boundaries today as well. These biscuits on yoghurt are perfect for showing how tectonic plates move. We added some food colouring to make the yoghurt red so as to represent the Earth's mantle. While moving the biscuits, we also touched a little on how the movement of plates causes earthquakes, volcanoes, and mountains. It's a simple but fun way for a child to learn about the three main types of plate boundaries."

This edible plate tectonics lesson idea is originally from @playdoughtoplato

@onesparkacademy

"As we near the end of the world geography lessons and prepare for the final map later this month, these incredible students are staying motivated and working HARD. Right now, we are finishing up our studies of Oceania. Last week, we learned about Kiribati and how climate change is impacting the ability of citizens to remain on their home islands (We also learned that Kiribati is the only nation that lies on all four hemispheres).

Today, we learned about the indigenous people of Papua New Guinea and some of what makes their food culture unique, we took a tour of Uluru (Ayer's Rock), one of the most remote tourist attractions on Earth, and we learned that the Great Barrier Reef is more than 1,250 miles long, has about 2,800 separate coral reef systems, and makes up about 10% of the world's coral. Next week, we'll learn more about the science behind coral bleaching due to climate change."

@bighousetinyhumans

The tactile materials, animals, and accessories that you put out with an interactive "geography tray" can be rotated out to represent different lands, biomes, and geographic features as you explore different types of landforms and life across the globe.

@homeeducation.blog

Students can model the physical features of a continent with air-drying modeling clay.

wanderlust
+ creativity

ART

Designer Christie Russert blends vibrant, abstract patterns and landscapes into designs that evoke positivity.

Her artwork, designed under her *Sunshine Canteen* brand, is influenced by travel.

Christie takes the creativity, spirit, and energy that comes from her travels and channels it into art that embodies a "sunshine state of mind."

Christie Russert
@sunshinecanteen
sunshinecanteen.com

sunshine canteen

"Was there a way that I could combine all my passions into one place?"

"When I create, it brings me to a happy place. I want to inspire that laid-back, sunny mentality into everyday life through my artwork."

Making art simply brings me joy. It is my meditation and passion in life. I view it as a long, steady mountain climb that I make small steps on daily.

Creative can mean so many things. It doesn't always mean your craft, or primary creative medium. Creative can mean painting, cooking a meal, or rearranging a closet. At a young age I was inspired by the design-rich subculture of snowboarding and skateboarding. At age 13 I remember going into my local ski shop and seeing all of the cool bold graphics on snowboards, stickers, and apparel — I was hooked. That's what inspired me to get into graphic design and study that in college.

I officially launched Sunshine Canteen in the fall of 2017, but it had been something I'd been dreaming about for many years. As a creative, it is often hard to pin down exactly what you want to do and how you want to execute. Too many interests and ideas had always kept distracting my vision. I always have loved pattern design and illustration, photography, skateboarding, camping & the outdoors, vintage & flea markets, and travel. Was there a way that I could combine all my passions into one place? That fall I decided that it was time to organize my thoughts and bring things into fruition.

I've always been into incorporating nature into my work. I have gotten more comfortable with color experimentation and abstraction and that has slowly evolved the style of my work.

Currently I use my kitchen table as my makeshift office space. I use a laptop and an iPad so I have the freedom to move around. I love working in coffee shops when I can.

My work is about 75% digital. I use my iPad and computer for the majority of my illustration work. When I use analog mediums like marbling, collage, or photography, I scan in my work and then alter using photoshop.

Strategies for Your Own Creative Endeavors

To get the creativity flowing, go to the library or bookstore, open a random book, and find inspiration in unexpected places and topics!

It also helps to dedicate certain times of the day to certain creative tasks. I personally like to draw and sketch new ideas in the evening as I wind down. It is relaxing and a good meditative practice for me. I like to dedicate the morning hours to work on emails and more business-type creative tasks when I have my coffee in hand.

Make sure that your workspace is nurturing by using lighting, plants & artwork. Lighting is a huge factor. I need to be in a space that has warm, natural bright light. I also love having plants and greenery to help freshen the air. I also like to have inspirational artwork and imagery around me.

I have a very structured way of working and also a totally loose way. It depends on the project and my mood. If it is more structured I'll gather inspiration (photos, colors, found items) and create a mood board. I take that and pull colors, draw motifs, and continue until I feel I have something interesting to work with. I also like to work in a less structured way and just free-flow draw and see where it takes me.

It helps to not beat yourself up when you try to accomplish everything at once and then fail -- that's when you burn out! Be happy if you can do at least one creative thing in a day.

Getting Inspired for the Next Big Thing

I take a ton of photos! I'm constantly snapping pics on my phone and on my camera. I also love to collect things on travels – business cards, stickers, pieces of paper, prints, etc. I have a GIANT bulletin board in my house that is essentially a huge growing collage of inspiration. It is my real life Pinterest board!

I love to read. I go back and forth between fiction and non-fiction. I also am a huge collector of books on art, photography, and architecture. One of my favorite pastimes is going to the local used book store. I love treasure hunting. If I were to pick some favorites from this year, they would be *Wild Game* and *A Star is Bored*.

My Top 5 LIFE TIPS

1 >> Take a walk and explore your own neighborhood. You will be surprised how much you notice when you slow down.

2 >> It may feel super good to cross things off the list, but being productive isn't everything. Slowing down is just as important.

3 >> It's ok to leave the dishes until the morning.

4 >> Coffee makes everything better.

5 >> Making the leap to do something new is scary, but it is also the most rewarding in the long run.

Exploring a new or favorite place is what fills my soul. My heart skips a beat when I can visit a place with fresh eyes, have my camera in hand, and soak in inspiration.

It helps to not beat yourself up when you try to accomplish everything at once and then fail... Be happy if you can do at least one creative thing in a day.

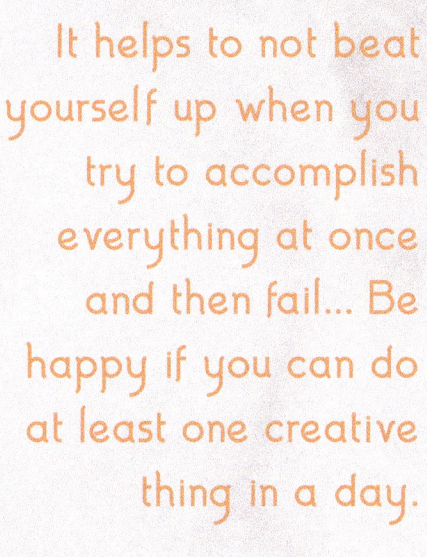

FAITH fueled TEACHING

by Shelda Raymonvil
@FaithFueledTeaching

A Guide to Fitting God Into Your Teaching Day

1. Read your Bible and pray before your students enter your classroom.

2. Listen to worship music while you're eating lunch or during your planning time.

3. Write your favorite scriptures on notes to stick around your personal area (desktop, laptop, notebook...)

4. Set alarms that will continue to redirect your focus on God.

5. Create a space in your teacher planner, next to your to-do list, dedicated to thanking God.

I didn't always consider myself a faith fueled teacher. When I first started teaching I kept my faith and teaching separate because I was more focused on mastering the art of teaching while also figuring out my life as a full time working adult (I was fresh out of college!). It wasn't until my 3rd year of teaching that I started to realize my faith shouldn't only be revealed on Sundays and be reflected in prayers before eating or going to sleep. That year, I started becoming very involved in my church and held leadership positions which led to a shift in my lifestyle.

I was determined to put God first and make Him the top priority in my life. So I started setting timers for myself throughout the work day with encouraging messages like "Close your eyes and ask God for peace" or "Don't forget to say a short prayer". After a while I stopped setting those timers because it all became natural for me! That's how my faith fueled teaching journey first began. Fast forward to my 8th year teaching and my faith fueled teaching journey has evolved. As I've grown in my relationship with God, my teaching lifestyle has grown. Now, being a faith fueled teacher means asking the Lord for guidance before planning a lesson, teaching a lesson, and reteaching a lesson.

Being a faith fueled teacher means praying for district leadership, administration, staff, students, families, and the school year. Being a faith fueled teacher means applying what the Bible says to all aspects of teaching. Being a faith fueled teacher means leading my class with the love of God fueling my heart. Being a faith fueled teacher means going to God in prayer when things get tough and when I may feel like giving up. Being a faith fueled teacher means being a light that shines so bright that others can see God through me!

Creativity
God gave us our own creativity so we can share in the joy that comes from Him who is the creator of the world! If we look all the way to the beginning of the bible, Genesis 1 verse 1, it says, "In the beginning God CREATED the heavens and the earth." He existed before all and created all! He even created us in His own image, to be like Him (Genesis 1:27).

God shows us how we, as creators, should live our lives. He spent His time creating for days. He assessed his creations frequently and saw them as good. When He finished His creations, He re-evaluated them all and deemed it VERY good. God even rested when He finished all the work that He did. Why not take on some of the good habits of our Father? Work hard. Assess. Rest. Repeat.

Paul also gives us guidelines on how we should live in 1 Thessalonians 4:11. It says we should aspire to lead a quiet life, mind our own business, and work with our hands. Sometimes we can get "stuck," unmotivated, or frustrated while creating but if we continue to seek the Lord's help through our quiet time, refrain from comparing ourselves to others and what they're doing, and focus on creating things for His glory, we can stay the course knowing that He will see us through!

My particular interest in creating jewelry stemmed from the simple fact that I love wearing jewelry and was determined to learn how to make my own! I didn't realize how much I enjoyed it until I started working on developing unique pieces. I felt like I was developing different personalities for each piece that I created. Each jewelry piece even has a name and a purpose! I found joy in creating something that would give all the glory to God which is why I started with the name Faith Fueled Jewelry.

When I created Faith Fueled Jewelry I knew I wanted it to reflect my love for God, my love for creating, and my love for education. With that being said, 5%

of each purchase is donated to organizations aimed towards supporting children, families, and education. It brings me complete joy to not only provide people with some arm candy but to be also giving back to others and giving glory to God!

Traveling the Globe
My love for traveling stems from my elementary education and my family travels. I was in an IB (International Baccalaureate) magnet program during my elementary school years where we studied culture and languages from around the world throughout the school year. On top of that, my parents took us to countries in the Caribbean to visit family when I was growing up. These fueled my love for traveling and appreciating different cultures.

I've only traveled to 9 countries so far and I spent at least 2 weeks in each of those countries so I could learn as much as possible about their culture, language, and customs (I do plenty of research before traveling as well). Learning about different cultures in the actual country has truly opened my eyes in seeing the beauty in all of our differences. Our differences make us who we are and make us all unique. Thus, we should learn about our differences, embrace our differences, and accept our differences.

Furthermore, I feel like another area of my brain has been unlocked after I've spent days at a time in a country. There's just so much to learn and appreciate! I also intentionally live among the locals to gain a true experience and love for a specific country. It makes me realize that there is so much more left for me to learn and so much more of the world left for me to explore, even as I grow older. There is never a time where you stop learning.

My first solo backpacking trip in Europe was a life changing experience for me. I challenged myself to take that leap of faith and travel by myself internationally because I was (and still am) a quiet, timid, and introverted person. I did extensive research before taking the 7 week trip especially because I was aware of being a Black, young, woman that would be traveling alone. I, unfortunately, had to consider how my identity would be perceived in a foreign place.

Nonetheless, I made the trip with no regrets whatsoever! I backpacked from Madrid then explored cities south of Spain (Granada, Sevilla, Cordoba), went to Barcelona, then decided to explore Italy (Rome, Pisa, Florence) because I met an Italian who encouraged me to make the trip (spur of the moment!). I lived in many hostels where I met other backpackers from all over the world! I had a general idea of where I wanted to go before taking the trip, but the recommendations from locals dictated how I spent my days: what I should do, see, and eat.

That experience taught me how to be more social, showed me how other people perceive me, and forced me to practice the main language. I had to depend on myself and discern what things I should and shouldn't do. I gained another level of confidence that I never knew I had. I've learned more things about myself traveling alone than I did traveling with other people. I've become more fearless and more aware of myself and my surroundings. It was the experience of a lifetime!

Follow me on Instagram @FaithFueledTeaching, follow me on YouTube (Faith Fueled Teaching), and check out my shop at faithfueledjewelry.com

Scripture Verses for Educators

"And the Lord's servant must not be quarrelsome but must be kind to everyone, able to teach, not resentful."

2 Timothy 2:24 NIV

"Let all that you do be done with love."

1 Corinthians 16:14 NKJV

"Trust in the Lord with all your heart and lean not on your own understanding; in all your ways acknowledge Him, and He shall direct your paths."

Proverbs 3:5-6 NKJV

"Do not be afraid--I am with you! I am your God--let nothing terrify you! I will make you strong and help you; I will protect you and save you."

Isaiah 41:10 GNTD

"Rejoice always, pray without ceasing, in everything give thanks; for this is the will of God in Christ Jesus for you."

1 Thessalonians 5:16-18 NKJV

"Draw near to God and He will draw near to you."

James 4:8

"Be anxious for nothing, but in everything by prayer and supplication, with thanksgiving, let your requests be made known to God; and the peace of God, which surpasses all understanding, will guard your hearts and minds through Christ Jesus."

Philippians 4:6-7 NKJV

Combine art, culture, and history by teaching your students about Australian Aboriginal Dot art. Its rich history in storytelling is fascinating. Explore the meaning behind different features of authentic Aboriginal art, and share with your students the fact that the artists must receive permission to paint a certain story through dot art. They may only paint a story that belongs to them through family.

Once you have covered the basics and talked about respecting the original culture, your own class can try these variations on authentic dot art. Its modern application is a crafty endeavor that is approachable for all ages. Even the youngest hands can give it a try.

aboriginal
DOT ART

Project #1

Trace a large circle on cardstock. Look at the samples of different dot-art patterns like the ones shown to the left. Select a style (or develop your own) and decorate with dots to create a pattern for a turtle shell. Add a head, legs, and a tail using marker. Each student will have his/her own unique turtle shell pattern.

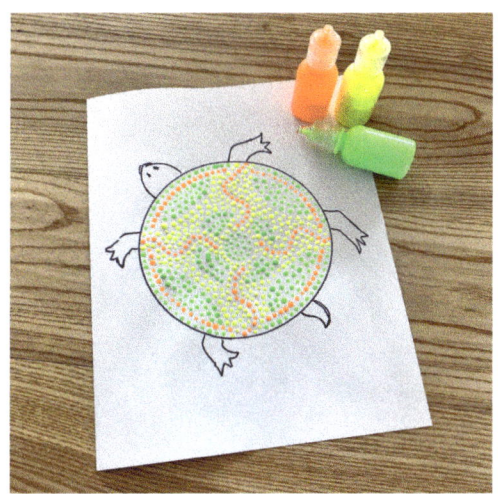

Project #2

Use dot paint to decorate flowerpots, t-shirts, or vases as a gift for parents. Even young students can create a beautiful and useful work of art with this method. Small squeeze bottles of paint are easiest for little hands to manage. Inexpensive terra cotta pots or tote bags are perfect surfaces to experiment with dot art patterns.

Project #3

Order some large sheets of Japanese rice paper. (They are not expensive.) Older students can create custom artwork for the home by using a small paintbrush and playing with different dot art designs and variations. When framed, the texture of the rice paper offers the appeal of high-end artwork.

"NEW SCHOOL"

Canterbury, Kent
@newschoolcanterbury
by Beth Cuenco

rooted in *values* and nestled on a *bio-dynamic farm*

MISSION & VALUES

New School inspires a love of learning and has each child's wellbeing at its heart. We nurture creative, compassionate, critical thinkers ready to meet the challenges and embrace the opportunities within our changing world.

As a community, we hold our values with great care and ensure that they inform our decisions and the way we all engage with each other and the wider world. It is deeply important to us that we not only teach these values but also offer an example of striving to live with them in our hearts.

school tour

NURTURING *creative* THINKERS

Many of the children of today will, in adult life, be employed as part of a workforce in jobs which have yet to be invented. It is therefore of the utmost importance that they are supported by an education that nurtures creativity, curiosity, compassion, and critical thinking skills, because it is these that will enable our children to embrace both the challenges and opportunities in this fast changing world.

Waldorf schools are sometimes erroneously seen as art schools because of the depth of the fine, practical, and performing arts that are woven in an interdisciplinary fashion among all the subjects. The creative arts are valued as highly as academic subjects and are also the language through which the more academic subjects are brought to life for children in our school. This method also ensures that each child is respected and supported in the way that they learn, whether they are visual, auditory, or kinesthetic learners.

Each lesson, whether a modern foreign language lesson, a science lesson, or a mathematics lesson, is taught creatively. Depending on the age of the children the lesson may include stories, song, drawing, or movement as an important part of enlivening the learning and placing it within the context of the world around us.

We offer an unhurried education that allows space for the children to question and follow their inquisitive minds – finding their own answers to life's big questions. This helps them develop their own sense of self and is also increasingly important in an age when the line between fiction and fact is so blurred and questioning is so essential.

BUILDING STRONG *character*

So many children today suffer from anxiety, stress, and serious mental health disorders, and very few of them receive the help they need. It is important now more than ever that young people are provided with a nurturing environment and are supported to develop the skills to become self-directed, emotionally stable, social beings.

In Waldorf Education, special attention is given to the child's whole being -- head, heart, and hands – with the heart being the emotional core.

the whole child – head, heart, and hands

Learning self-regulation, listening skills, empathy, patience, and kindness toward others is considered an essential part of each child's education for life.

Stories play an important role in encouraging children to use their imaginations and to develop empathy and understanding for others whilst inquiry-based learning helps them connect emotionally to their learning and to understand the influences that their own unique experiences have on their mindsets.

Empathy and care are modeled within the community and encouraged everyday. In many Waldorf Schools the Class teacher stays with the children from Class One through to Class Eight (for us this is Class 5 because we currently only go up to class five). The Class Teacher has the Class for the first lesson of every day as well as some additional lessons across the day.

Other subject lessons bring additional expertise on modern foreign languages, movement, storytelling, and craft. The class teacher develops a strong relationship with the children and their families, understanding their home life and backgrounds, believing in each child's unique potential, and responding to their developmental needs. This provides the children with a beautiful model of empathetic leadership within the classroom community.

At New School, our values of Mutual Respect, Kindness, Active Listening, Safety, and Best Effort are rooted in how we behave each and every day. Through bringing these values to life in an authentic way, we not only see direct benefits in the classroom and school community but hope to ultimately help foster a better, kinder world.

PRIORITIZING CORE *values*

Mutual Respect: I will treat others with respect at all times and can expect to be treated with respect by others, at all times.

Attentive Listening: When another is speaking, I listen. Listening means not talking, not interrupting, not ignoring, and looking at, as well as listening to, the other. We listen with our whole selves, not just our ears.

Kindness: Kindness is how we treat ourselves, others, and our environment, every day. Appreciations are what we do, put-downs are what we do not do. Appreciations are things we say to or do for others that make them feel good; put-downs are things that, if said to or done to others, would not. Actions or words that are unkind are unacceptable.

Best Effort: In all activities and at each moment I will do my best. This applies to my work in class and my interactions with others. By doing my best at all times I can feel proud of who I strive to be and feel that my contribution to the community is of great value.

Safety: We honour our own safety and the well-being of others.

nature AND LAND CARE

We are incredibly lucky that we have the most beautiful site in an Area of Outstanding Natural Beauty, surrounded by a bio-dynamic farm. Children of all ages take part in caring for the site and learning how we can make the most of what nature provides.

Landcare lessons work through practical experience to develop a sense within each child, that as human beings, we draw our daily sustenance from the earth, and therefore have responsibilities toward the earth both for our sake and for the well-being of others.

As the children develop through Kindergarten and into the Lower School, wonder awakes responsibility, which ripens into love for the world around us. Practical gardening skills strengthen hope and our ability to make a positive difference to the world. Whilst the development of knowledge and skills are important, the purpose of these lessons is not to train the children to become gardeners, but rather to nurture a deeper appreciation for and connection with the natural world.

The children take great pride in participating in the production of the food they eat. From seeds to seedlings and from planting to harvest, the students weed, water, and tend to vegetables, herbs, flowers, and fruits. They enjoy harvesting and learning to prepare what they have grown – and then eating it! Coming full circle, scraps

pride in the land

from meals are composted, and students use that compost to renew the topsoil of the gardens.

The experience of caring for the land develops positive habits for life, like the importance of inner strength and willpower that helps us get on with tasks not because we enjoy them, but because they are necessary. It allows for recognition that for a healthy site we need healthy cooperation between each other, between ourselves and nature, and between the different natural forces on the site itself. This leads to an awareness of the parts of life working together to form a whole.

LESSONS IN *nature*

Bees:
The very best thing we can do to help ensure the survival of bees is to plant the flowers they need to nourish them. Children of all ages are helping to make our school a pollinator-friendly site, bursting with wildflowers and herbs: borage, goldenrod, poppies, lilac, lavender, mint, sunflowers, and many more. These plants attract not only bees but also butterflies and other pollinators.

Composting:
Over this last year we have built compost bins for our leaf mulch and our raw food-waste. This coming year we are hoping to raise the funds for a hot composter so that scraps from meals are composted, and the children can then use that compost to renew the topsoil of the gardens.

Composting provides a responsible way to reuse waste and teaches children about the natural cycles of life, death, rebirth, and the recycling of nutrients in the ecosystem. It also reminds children that they are part of a bigger picture and that what they do really matters.

Through composting their waste, our children are taking a step to care for our environment and give back to the garden. Just as each microorganism deep within the compost pile individually is small, when all the organisms work together they are able to decompose large amounts of waste and contribute beautiful, rich soil to the garden.

"IF YOU DESIGN A SYSTEM TO DO SOMETHING SPECIFIC, DON'T BE SURPRISED IF IT DOES IT. IF YOU RUN AN EDUCATION SYSTEM BASED ON STANDARDISATION AND CONFORMITY, WHICH SUPPRESSES INDIVIDUALITY, IMAGINATION, AND CREATIVITY, DON'T BE SURPRISED IF THAT'S WHAT IT DOES."
>> KEN ROBINSON

THE *challenges* WE FACE

Even though the curricula have developed, the essence of our mainstream education system has stayed the same with children being taught in a standardised way and taught what to think rather than how to think. This outdated system of education was designed to meet the needs of the Industrial Revolution but is inherently unsuited to the world today. Ken Robinson summed this up perfectly when he said:

"If you design a system to do something specific, don't be surprised if it does it. If you run an education system based on standardisation and conformity, which suppresses individuality, imagination, and creativity, don't be surprised if that's what it does."

In Kent, many children sit the Kent Test, an examination administered in their last year of Primary School (aged 10 - 11) to determine their admission to Grammar School and other secondary schools that use academic selection. This puts immense pressure on children at this critical age and can lead to disappointment and deep-rooted feelings of failure.

Cognitive researchers point out that children's emotional health affects their academic performance, and their academic performance affects their emotional health. In other words, depression, anxiety, and unhappiness can impair educational performance and feelings of failure contribute to emotional health problems.

We know that curiosity and an eagerness to learn are innate qualities within us but yet this hunger for learning so often becomes dulled as children progress through an education system that prioritizes an ability to pass exams over our children's emotional wellbeing and the nurturing of a lifelong love of learning.

best effort

5 Ways to Style an OVERSIZED CARDIGAN

CARMEN MYER @THEGOODCARMABLOG

My advice to women shopping on a strict budget or those who are just beginning to use a capsule wardrobe is to invest in good quality pieces, that you absolutely love and that can be worn in many different ways. One of those pieces for me is this cardigan/sweater dress. I love everything about it: the length, the chunky knit, the color, the dramatic sleeves, the tortoiseshell buttons...everything! I can wear it for date night, to work, running errands, and out to dinner with friends and still never tire of it. This was one of the five clothing items I purchased last year during the months of October-December and I'm so glad I did. I hope to take advantage of its versatility and warmth in fall seasons to come. I enjoy making new outfits from the items I already have in my closet and encourage you to get creative with what you already have! You'll be surprised at what you come up with.

A Twist on a Classic

Jeans and a white tee never go out of style. Adding something unexpected, like this oversized cardigan elevates the entire look.

With a Dress!

Layering is key in the colder months, and this is a simple way to get more wear out of your favorite dresses. If you have a shorter dress you want to wear, you can add tights or a pair of warm boots.

Buttoned Up with Boots

Over the knee boots have been everywhere the past few years. I swoon over a cute sweater dress paired with boots every time. This look is perfect for a night out with your friends or partner.

4 Belting a dress never fails to add that extra pizazz and polish. I would suggest doing this if you have a sweater dress that is a bit looser and you want it to be more form fitting.

Belt it!

I hope this gives you some ideas and is the catalyst for a weekend of wardrobe exploration. Have fun getting dressed! Xo, Carmen

All Black

5 This is a simple way to look chic when you have minimal time to get ready. I paired a black bodysuit with my favorite pair of faux leather leggings and felt extra cute! Add a red lip and this combination would be complete!

Inspiration from...

DESMOND TUTU

Inclusive, good quality education is a foundation for dynamic and equitable societies.

How could you have a soccer team if we were all goalkeepers? How would it be an orchestra if all were french horns?

Children are a wonderful gift. They have an extraordinary capacity to see into the heart of things and to expose sham and humbug for what they are.

Exclusion is never the way forward on our shared paths to freedom and justice.

It is our moral obligation to give every child the very best education possible.

The price of freedom is eternal vigilance.

If you want peace, you don't talk to your friends. You talk to your enemies.

You stand out in the crowd only because you have these many, many carrying you on their shoulders.

Quotes from Archbishop Desmond Tutu

www.ingramcontent.com/pod-product-compliance
Lightning Source LLC
Chambersburg PA
CBHW042038100526
44587CB00030B/4480